1. THE REFORMER/ PERFECTIONIST
2. THE HELPER/GIVER/ LOVER
3. THE ACHIEVER/ MOTIVATOR
4. THE INDIVIDUALIST/ARTIST/ ROMANTIC
5. THE INVESTIGATOR/THINKER/ OBSERVER
6. THE SKEPTIC/DOUBTER/LOYALIST
7. THE ENTHUSIAST/ ADVENTURER/ GENERALIST
8. THE LEADER/ CHALLENGER/PROTECTOR
9. THE PEACEMAKER/ MEDIATOR

Headstart for Happiness

A Guide Book Using Kundalini Yoga and the Enneagram

Lynn

Headstart for Happiness

*A Guide Book Using Kundalini Yoga
and the Enneagram*

Published 2016
Printed in the United States of America and Greece
ISBN: 978-0-9971831-0-8

For information, please contact:
Rasayan Center, LLC
PO Box 7775
San Francisco, CA 94120

Copyright
Lynn Roulo and Rasayan Center, LLC 2016

Copyright
The Teachings of Yogi Bhajan 2016

All rights reserved. No part of this publication may be reproduced, distributed, or transmitted in any form or by any means, including photocopying, recording, digital scanning, or other electronic or mechanical methods, without the prior written permission of the publisher, except in the case of brief quotations embodied in critical reviews and certain other noncommercial uses permitted by copyright law. For permission requests, please contact Lynn Roulo through www.lynnroulo.com.

Acknowledgements:

While the Enneagram material and content in this manual is my original work, the information about the Enneagram system is based on the work of the following authors (listed alphabetically):

- Beatrice Chestnut
- Russ Hudson
- Peter O'Hanrahan
- Helen Palmer
- Don Riso

The quotes referenced from people in the Enneagram type chapters are paraphrased from over 100 narrative tradition panels I attended and from personal discussion with people who felt clear in their identification as their Enneagram type.

The information from The Teachings of Yogi Bhajan has been reviewed for accuracy by KRI.

All teachings, yoga sets, techniques, kriyas and meditations courtesy of The Teachings of Yogi Bhajan. Reprinted with permission. Unauthorized duplication is a violation of applicable laws. ALL RIGHTS RESERVED. No part of these Teachings may be reproduced or transmitted in any form by any means, electronic or mechanical, including photocopying and recording, or by any information storage and retrieval system, except as may be expressly permitted in writing by the The Teachings of Yogi Bhajan. To request permission, please write to KRI at PO Box 1819, Santa Cruz, NM 87567 or see www.kriteachings.org.

Always consult your physician before beginning this or any other exercise program. Nothing in this book is to be construed as medical advice. Neither the author nor the publisher shall be liable or responsible for any loss, injury or damage allegedly arising from any information or suggestion in this book. The benefits attributed to the practice of Kundalini Yoga and meditation stem from centuries-old yogic tradition. Results will vary with individuals.

Headstart for Happiness

*A Guide Book Using Kundalini Yoga
and the Enneagram*

Lynn

CONTENTS

1. THE REFORMER/ PERFECTIONIST
2. THE HELPER/GIVER/ LOVER
3. THE ACHIEVER/ MOTIVATOR
4. THE INDIVIDUALIST/ARTIST/ ROMANTIC
5. THE INVESTIGATOR/THINKER/ OBSERVER
6. THE SKEPTIC/DOUBTER/LOYALIST
7. THE ENTHUSIAST/ ADVENTURER/ GENERALIST
8. THE LEADER/ CHALLENGER/PROTECTOR
9. THE PEACEMAKER/ MEDIATOR

INTRODUCTION 11

THE ENNEAGRAM SYSTEM OF PERSONALITY 13

   Overview 13

   Level 1: The Nine Types 17

   Level 2: The Three Centers 21

   Level 3: The Wings 23

   Level 4: The Subtypes 24

   Level 5: Security Points/Stress Points 26

KUNDALINI YOGA 29

   Overview 29

   Kundalini Yoga Glossary of Terms 36

THE REFORMER/PERFECTIONIST
ENNEAGRAM TYPE ONE 41

   Kriya for Heart Connection 47

   Meditation to Burn Inner Anger and Build the Immune System 52

THE HELPER/GIVER/LOVER
ENNEAGRAM TYPE TWO 55

   Kriya for Balancing Praana and Apaana 61

   Meditation for a Calm Heart 65

THE ACHIEVER/MOTIVATOR
ENNEAGRAM TYPE THREE 67

   Kriya for Balancing the Head and the Heart 73

   Meditation To Change the Ego 77

THE INDIVIDUALIST/ARTIST/ROMANTIC
ENNEAGRAM TYPE FOUR 79
Kriya for Strengthening the Aura 85
Meditation for Inner Conflict Resolver Reflex 88

THE INVESTIGATOR/THINKER/OBSERVER
ENNEAGRAM TYPE FIVE 91
Kriya to Balance and Recharge the Nervous and Immune System 97
Wahe Guru Meditation 101

THE SKEPTIC/DOUBTER/LOYALIST
ENNEAGRAM TYPE SIX 103
Kriya for Emotional and Mental Balance 109
Meditation for Caliber for Constant Self-Authority 113

THE ENTHUSIAST/ADVENTURER/GENERALIST
ENNEAGRAM TYPE SEVEN 115
Kriya To Purify The Self 121
Caliber of Life Meditation 126

THE LEADER/CHALLENGER/PROTECTOR
ENNEAGRAM TYPE EIGHT 129
Kriya to Open the Heart 135
One Minute Breath Meditation 141

THE PEACEMAKER/MEDIATOR
ENNEAGRAM TYPE NINE 143
The Wake Up Series 149
Breath of Fire Meditation 152

CLOSING 155

CONTENTS

*"You can never hide from your truth.
If you do, you will always be lost."*

~Yogi Bhajan

INTRODUCTION

1+1=3

Synergy: *the interaction of elements or systems that when combined produce a total effect that is greater than the sum of the individual elements.*

This book combines two complete systems, the Enneagram System of Personality[1] and Kundalini Yoga as taught by Yogi Bhajan[2] to accomplish just that.

Imagine you are lost in the wilderness and trying to find your way out. You may have a map to help you navigate, but you won't go far if you are too weak or tired. Or you have plenty of energy, strength and supplies but no map so you don't know where to go. Life is often like that—you know you want change, but something holds you back. Either you aren't clear about your new direction, or you know the direction, but you just don't move towards the change you want.

This book provides the map of the Enneagram and the strength, energy and supplies of Kundalini Yoga to help you out of the wilderness.

---

[1] *Enneagram in this manual refers to Enneagram System of Personality*
[2] *Kundalini Yoga in this manual refers to Kundalini Yoga as taught by Yogi Bhajan®.*

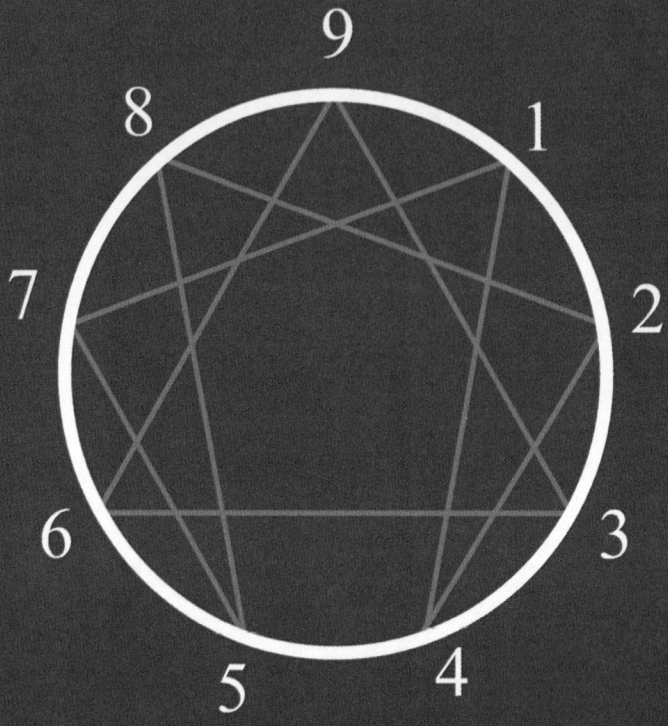

"If we could look into each other's hearts and understand the unique challenges each of us faces, I think we would treat each other much more gently, with more love, patience, tolerance and care."

~Marvin J. Ashton

THE ENNEAGRAM SYSTEM OF PERSONALITY

 **Overview**

What is the Enneagram?

The Enneagram is a system of human personality that helps explain why people behave the way they do. It is essentially a map of personality, behavior and motivation. It has been referred to as the "GPS of wisdom." I think of it as a tool for compassion.

The Enneagram says our experience in life is governed by a central question:

Where does your attention go?

You can think of it like a magnifying glass, and the question becomes "Where does your magnifying glass point?" In other words, what is your attention drawn to—what is your attention bias?

Once you learn your attention bias, your own behavior begins to make more sense. And once you learn the Enneagram type of someone else, his or her behavior begins to make more sense. This attention bias also explains how two people can be in the same situation and have radically different interpretations of what happened.

The Enneagram says our attention goes to one of nine general places. These places are given names and numbers and referred to as Enneagram types. Each of the nine

Enneagram types can be thought of as a country of personality with its own cultural bias. For example, two Americans can hear the word "Thanksgiving" and will have a similar understanding of the American holiday. Two Finnish people may hear the same word and have no understanding of the holiday, as it isn't part of their culture. Two Enneagram Type Fives will have a similar understanding of the need for time alone each day. And two Enneagram Type Sevens might have little or no understanding of the need for time alone each day as it isn't part of their attention bias.

The Enneagram recognizes that each person has his or her own history and life experience, unique family dynamics and upbringing and his or her own emotional makeup. This personal fingerprint is not Enneagram specific. However, much like the country analogy, the Enneagram provides a framework for attention similarities and differences. And it helps explain why two people of the same Enneagram type, while possibly having widely varying backgrounds and personal experience, will have similar motivations and similar emotional blueprints. Each person remains a totally unique individual, but they will share a focus of attention with other people of their Enneagram type.

Where does the Enneagram come from?
- 2000 B.C.: References to the Enneagram symbol are seen in ancient Mesopotamia.
- 1920s: Russian philosopher G.I. Gurdjieff began writing about the system, referring to the three centers of the head, heart and body (see more about this later in the chapter).
- 1960s: Bolivian-born Oscar Ichazo began writing about the system and specifically the nine different personality profiles.
- 1970s: Claudio Naranjo, a Chilean-born, American-trained psychiatrist, learned the system from Ichazo and began teaching it in the United States.
- 1980s: American authors Helen Palmer, Don Riso and Russ Hudson (among others) began writing mainstream books about the Enneagram.

While the symbol of the Enneagram has references back to ancient Mesopotamia, the rediscovery of the system and its entry into the mainstream are largely credited to Gurdjieff, Ichazo and Naranjo.

Gurdjieff, born in the late 1800s, is one of the first people to directly reference the Enneagram. Gurdjieff began writing about the system as part of a larger body of work called "The Fourth Way." He cited many sources for his material but primarily credited esoteric Christianity. He brought the symbol of the Enneagram into the mainstream, but he didn't openly teach about the nine distinct personality types -focusing his teaching instead on the three centers.

Oscar Ichazo began teaching the core principles of the modern Enneagram as part of a larger system in the 1960s. Ichazo is vague about the origins of his work, but he references Aristotle and neo-Platonic sources, as well as his own various learnings and influences, which allowed him to develop some of the material himself.

Claudio Naranjo learned the system from Ichazo and began teaching the material in California in the United States. Naranjo used Ichazo's teaching along with his own training in a variety of other systems and methods to teach the system with more refinement and specificity around the nine personality types. His teachings and interpretations were used by a variety of American authors, and mainstream books about the Enneagram became available in the 1980s.

How do people use the Enneagram?

The Enneagram can be thought of as a tool for compassion and is used to help explain the behavior of people around you and to provide context for your own behavior. Many people breathe a great sigh of relief when they discover their Enneagram type because it helps them better understand their own behavior. They report:

> *"Now I can stop fighting with myself..."*
>
> *"It's like someone wrote a chapter about my psychology."*
>
> *"This has put a bandage on my heart..."*
>
> *"One Enneagram typing session was better than ten therapy sessions."*

More specifically, the system is used
- for personal development
- in the business world for team dynamics and communication
- in churches by clergy to provide better counseling to parishioners
- in creative writing classes for character development
- in relationship counseling to deepen interpersonal understanding

Learning Your Enneagram Type

An important aspect to the Enneagram is that you "self type," meaning you identify which of the nine types fits your own attention bias. The idea behind self-typing is that other people see your behavior but don't really know what is going on in your head. You are the only person who knows your own thoughts. The Enneagram speaks to motivation more than behavior so the reality is you are the only person who could ever say what type you are.

There are three main ways people discover their Enneagram type:
- They read the type information and self-identify.
- They have an Enneagram typing interview with someone certified in Enneagram typing.
- They take an Enneagram typing test.

For some people, their behavior is clear enough that the match to their type description is obvious to them. This is how it worked for me. I bought a book, read the types, and when I got to my type (I'm a Type Seven), I felt like someone had described me almost exactly. It was eerie.

Another way to discover your type is through an Enneagram typing interview. These interviews take between one and two hours and are designed to help you uncover your type with the assistance of a trained interviewer. The interviewer doesn't tell you your type but instead points you in the direction of type possibilities based on your answers.

Many people also take Enneagram typing tests (either online or in publications). These tests range from very general to very specific. I think the typing tests can be interesting, but I generally don't advise people to rely on them exclusively. The tests can be a useful tool to use in conjunction with either or both of the methods above.

Some people get confused self-typing when they fit most, but not all, of the type characteristics. But that's not the point. To align with a type, the idea is that you are most of the things, most of the time. It is rare that someone is 100 percent of his or her type traits 100 percent of the time.

 ## The Goal

"Life is simple. Life is not complicated. Life is only one thing: Identify yourself."
~Yogi Bhajan

The purpose of the Enneagram is not to change types or to stop being who you are. The goal is to learn your attention bias and learn to relax that attention habit. An attention bias is where your attention goes. An attention habit is how you act that out. Your attention bias won't change, but your attention habit can.

Whenever you have an attention habit, you lean forward towards that area of attention and away from its opposite. This brings you out of balance. Once the habit is relaxed, balance can be reestablished, and you can begin to choose your behavior. Without this choice, you are acting out automatically, much like a machine. When the habit is relaxed, you can act from conscious choice, not just react.

level 1:
THE NINE TYPES

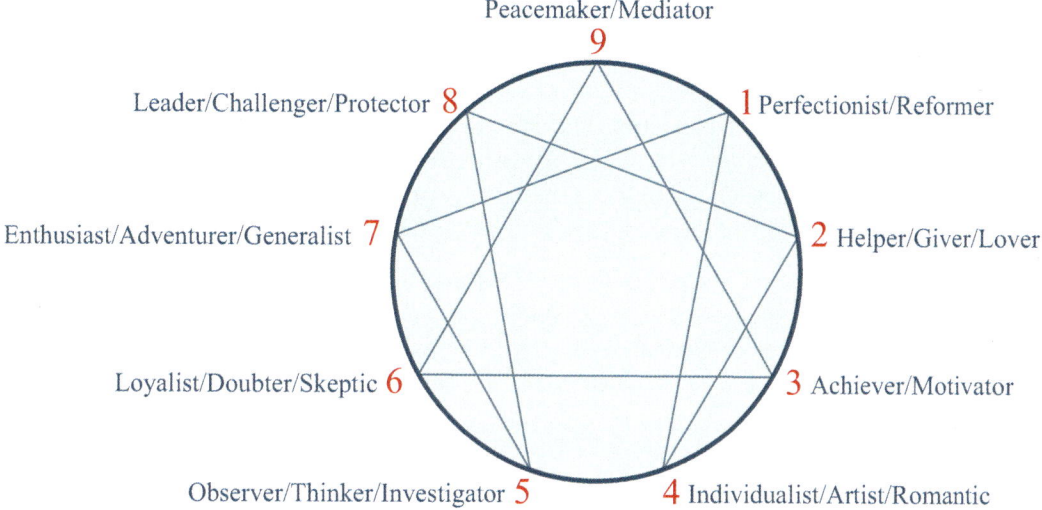

Each type has tremendous gifts to offer the world, and all types are valuable and important. There is no type that is better or worse than another. The goal of the Enneagram is to help you share your strengths, not your weaknesses.

"We don't see the world as it is, we see it as we are."
— Anaïs Nin

A brief description of the general behavior and attention biases of the nine types is below. Because each type sees the world through the magnifying lens of their attention bias, each type is experiencing the world very differently.

1) **Type One:** Perfectionist/Reformer
(seeks improvement and perfection/avoids leaving things as imperfect)

Perfectionists/Reformers are typically realistic, conscientious and principled. They strive to live up to their high ideals. This person sees the world in black and white, right and wrong, perfect and imperfect. It is difficult for them to leave things in an imperfect state.

Attention bias: The magnifying glass goes to what needs improvement.
They see what needs improvement or correction. Their attention moves away from the current state as good enough.

2) Type Two: Helper/Giver/Lover
(seeks satisfying the needs of others/avoids own needs)

Helpers/Givers/Lovers are typically warm, concerned, nurturing and sensitive to the needs, preferences and desires of the people around them. They proactively look for ways to be helpful, useful and likeable. This person is the stereotypical perfect host or hostess with an almost sixth sense for the needs of others. Type Twos typically report having boundary issues and having a very difficult time saying no to a request, even if they really don't want to do what is being asked of them.

Attention bias: The magnifying glass goes to the needs of others.
They see the wants and preferences of other people and work to gain their appreciation. This can manifest as offering help and assistance to others or to presenting themselves in a likeable manner. Their attention moves away from their own needs.

3) Type Three: Achiever/Motivator
(seeks success/avoids failure)

Achievers/Motivators are typically energetic, optimistic, self-assured and goal-oriented. Gifted at focusing on goals and achieving them, Type Three personifies the "human doing" rather than human being. This person is highly productive, efficient and can be extremely motivating to others. They want to be the best in any situation and can be overly concerned about the opinions of others.

Attention bias: The magnifying glass goes towards being successful in the eyes of other people. They see what brings success and approval from others. Their attention moves away from anything that could be recognized as failure, particularly in the eyes of others.

4) Type Four: Individualist/Artist/Romantic
(seeks individuality/avoids the ordinary)

Individualists/Artists/Romantics are original and authentic, with intense feelings spanning the entire emotional spectrum. They have felt great emotional highs, deep emotional lows and can feel everything in between on a daily basis. This person favors intensity (either positive or negative) to commonplace and routine. Drawn to what is missing, Type Fours spend a lot of time thinking about what they don't have and experiencing longing.

Attention bias: The magnifying glass goes to what is missing, distant or unavailable. They see what they don't have and long for it. The darker emotions of sadness, despair and melancholy tend to feel familiar and comfortable. Their attention moves away from what they do have and from feelings of satisfaction and fulfillment.

5) Type Five: Observer/Thinker/Investigator
(seeks self sufficiency/avoids external demands)

Observers/Thinkers/Investigators are typically introverted, curious, analytical and insightful. These are the owls of the Enneagram with a very boundaried approach to life. This person is quite observant and curious but generally likes to observe from a distance, slightly out of the group. Eventually he or she gets bored or lonely and joins the group. But joining the group often provokes anxiety and brings a tendency to withdraw. They are constantly asking the question "Should I engage?" or "Should I withdraw?" Their instinct is to withdraw.

Attention bias: The magnifying glass goes to maintaining self-sufficiency. They see the expectations and the demands of the outside world and have a heightened awareness of personal resources (including time and energy). The central question they focus on is "What is required of me and do I have what it takes to deliver?" The attention moves towards concerns about scarcity and away from feelings of abundance and adequate resources.

6) Type Six: Loyalist/Doubter/Skeptic
(seeks security/avoids danger)

Loyalists/Doubters/Skeptics are typically responsible, reliable, trustworthy and value security and loyalty. Type Sixes are the African gazelles of the Enneagram—scanning and on high alert for danger at all times. This person can quickly and easily identify what could be dangerous or problematic in a situation and begins preparing for that outcome. Type Sixes also align with the values of duty and loyalty and often feel responsible to step in during challenging situations. It can be difficult for Type Sixes to believe in positive outcomes and more moderate scenarios.

Attention bias: The magnifying glass goes to potential danger and threats to security. They see hazards, pitfalls, risks and experience worst-case scenario thinking. They experience this thinking as vividly as a high-definition motion picture with the worst-case scenario unfolding before their eyes. Their attention moves away from more moderate potential outcomes or what could go right in a situation.

7) Type Seven: Enthusiast/Adventurer/Generalist
(seeks the positive/avoids the negative)

Enthusiasts/Adventurers/Generalists are typically energetic, lively, adventurous and optimistic. These are the experience junkies of the Enneagram—curious, positive and often bold, they are drawn to try almost anything they haven't done before. This person has a very easy time imagining what could go right and what could be amazing. He or she may have a very difficult time imagining what could go wrong. They frequently underestimate danger and sometimes get themselves into difficult situations because of this attention bias. Lack of focus and discernment is often a theme for Type Sevens.

 Attention bias: The magnifying glass goes to the positive.
They see what is pleasurable, fun, positive and new. They are attracted to possibility, and their attention is often in the future, planning enjoyable experiences. Their attention moves away from anything negative, painful or limiting.

8) Type Eight: Leader/Challenger/Protector
(seeks power/avoids vulnerability)

Leaders/Challengers/Protectors are typically resourceful, self-reliant, self-confident and protective. These are the soldiers of the Enneagram. Tough, direct, prepared for combat and comfortable with confrontation, this type instinctively understands power dynamics. This person projects a "what you see is what you get" attitude and tends to be very straight-forward, honest and blunt. Justice is usually a theme for Type Eights. They sometimes get feedback that they are "too much" or that their aggressive communication style is overwhelming to others. Expressing vulnerability is not easy for them.

 Attention bias: The magnifying glass goes to power.
They see power and power dynamics: who is in control, who is vulnerable and might need protection, and so on. They are quite comfortable challenging power and authority and will often step forward to protect the underdog. Their attention moves away from personal feelings of vulnerability and the softer emotions.

9) Type Nine: Peacemaker/Mediator
(seeks harmony/avoids conflict)

Peacemakers/Mediators are typically receptive, good-natured, supportive and soothing. Type Nines are gifted at understanding the viewpoints of others and are so good at leaning into other people's agendas and perspectives, they sometimes lose their sense of themselves. This is a person for whom tranquility is a main focus. They tend to be very conflict avoidant. Indecision, procrastination and stubbornness can be themes for Type Nine.

 Attention bias: The magnifying glass goes to harmony.
They see what it takes to maintain a smooth, peaceful environment. Their attention moves away from creating conflict of any type as conflict can be extremely anxiety-provoking for most Type Nines.

level 2:
THE THREE CENTERS

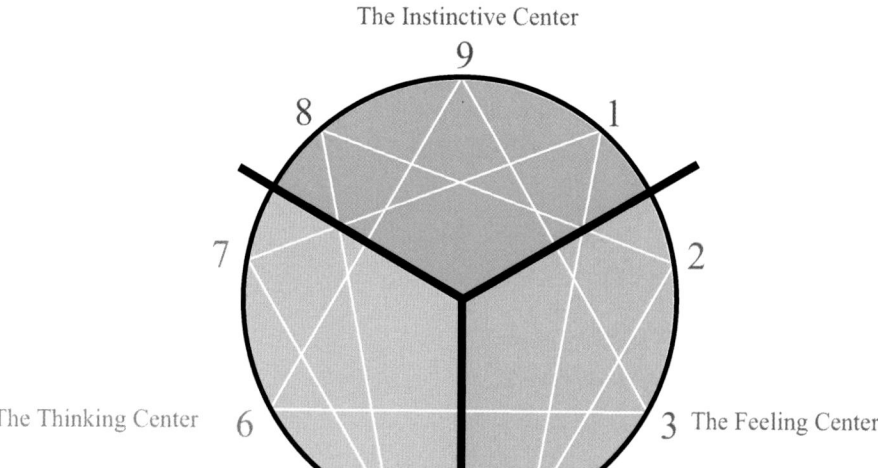

Within the Enneagram, the nine primary types are grouped into three centers. The centers determine physically and energetically how each of the types first receives information. Each center also points to a central psychological, sensitive issue--a pain point--facing the personality. The three centers and their related types are:

Center	Types
Heart / Feeling	2, 3, 4
Head / Thinking	5, 6, 7
Body / Instinctive	8, 9, 1

The Heart/Feeling Types
(Sensitive Issue: Sadness or Shame)

The heart/feeling types first receive information through their feelings and emotions. When new information is received, they feel it through the energy of emotion. The heart/feeling types all have a subconscious or background issue with sadness, grief or shame. These types all have themes around their image.

In all three centers, there is one primary type who under expresses the issue, one who over expresses the issue, and one who represses the issue. In the Heart/Feeling Types:

Type Two under expresses shame. Instead, Type Twos tend to express pride by presenting that they need very little themselves, and they are capable of meeting the needs of others.

Type Three represses shame. Type Threes deal with shame by repressing it and focusing instead on their successes and accomplishments.

Type Four over expresses shame. Type Fours overly identify with shame and subconsciously build it in as part of their identity. It is hard for them to objectively see their successes and accomplishments.

The Head/Thinking Types
(Sensitive Issue: Anxiety)

The head/thinking types first receive and process information through their intellect and mind. They process information mentally before the information flows to their feelings and their body. The central issue each of the head/thinking types deals with is anxiety.

Type Five under expresses anxiety. Type Fives gain relief from anxiety through information, research and isolation. When anxiety starts to build for Type Five, their tendency is to withdraw and recharge.

Type Six over expresses anxiety. For many Type Sixes, anxiety is a core part of their daily experience. They tend to feel anxiety regularly, often and at times quite intensely.

Type Seven represses anxiety. Type Sevens repress anxiety by staying on the go. As soon as anxiety starts to arise, they look to external stimuli for relief. It can be very difficult for Type Sevens to recognize their anxiety as it is experienced more as boredom or a desire for new experiences.

The Body/Instinctive Types
(Sensitive Issue: Anger)

The body/instinctive types first receive and process information through their bodies. They process information somatically before the information flows to their minds and emotions. The central issue each of the body types is dealing with is anger.

Type Eight over expresses anger. Type Eights tend to access anger easily and quickly. Their energy moves out towards their environment as a subconscious strategy to keep anything from getting too close to them. Slowing down the anger response can be a core growth opportunity for Type Eight.

Type Nine under expresses anger. Type Nines generally don't feel anger real time. They disassociate from anger and often feel it at some point in the future (sometimes years in the future). Energetically, Type Nines maintain external boundaries by allowing problematic things to go on so as not to disturb external harmony. They also maintain internal boundaries through denial of feelings that would disturb internal harmony. Type Nines expend a lot of energy maintaining all these boundaries against reality and sometime report fatigue.

Type One represses anger. Type Ones tend to deny feelings of anger and instead experience continual annoyance and irritation. Their energy moves towards the outside world, but they also spend energy maintaining a very strong internal boundary. This internal boundary is used to hold back certain unconscious impulses (for example, anger).

level 3: THE WINGS

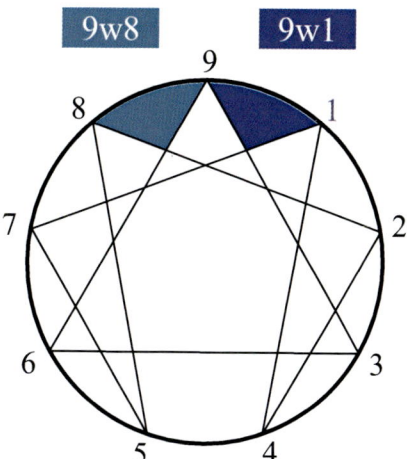

The Enneagram includes a third level of insight and nuance—the wings. Each primary type is influenced, or flavored, by one of the types next to it, called a wing. For example, an Enneagram Type Nine would have either an Eight wing or a One wing. While the motivations and drives remain aligned with the primary type, secondary motivations and behavior can be aligned with the wing. With this nuance, two people of the same primary type, but with different wings, can behave very differently.

People with strong "wing" influences can adopt many of the behaviors of their wing type. However, their drive and motivation still come from their primary type. For example, someone who is a Type Seven with a strong Type Eight wing may sometimes become very combative, direct, blunt and angry. However, the drive for fun and positive experiences remains the main drive, and the combative behavior is a secondary expression. The magnifying glass, or attention bias, remains on having positive experiences.

In Enneagram terms, the wings are denoted by a "w" and the wing number comes after the primary number. For example, a Type Nine with a Type Eight wing is written 9w8. A Type Nine with a Type One wing is written 9w1 and so on.

level 4: THE SUBTYPES[3]

Within the Enneagram there is a fourth level of insight—the subtypes.

The subtype describes your instinctual drive for how the world works. It isn't a conscious choice you make but rather an instinctive sense.

There are three distinct subtypes:
- The self-preservation subtype
- The social subtype
- The intimate subtype

---

[3] All Subtype information has been paraphrased from "The Complete Enneagram, 27 Paths to Greater Self Knowledge" by Beatrice Chestnut, PhD

These three subtypes apply to all nine of the primary Enneagram types. When combined with the primary type, there are in total 27 subtype variations.

Subtype	Emphasis	Worldview
Self-Preservation	Personal needs and interests	"I am responsible for myself, you are responsible for yourself, and we all understand these rules."
Social	Group or community interests	"The world functions better when we all get along."
Intimate	Intimate or one-on-one connections	"You and me against the world."

The subtype adds another layer of flavoring to each of the nine types. In some instances, the personality doesn't change that dramatically based on the subtype. Type Five, the Observer/Thinker/Investigator has similar external behavior across all three subtypes. In other types, the subtype changes the external behavior dramatically. Type Four, the Individualist/Artist/Romantic and Type Six, the Loyalist/Doubter/Skeptic behave dramatically differently based on the subtype.

A basic overview of the three subtypes is outlined below. More detailed explanations are included in the type chapters.

Self-preservation
The self-preservation drive has an instinct of "I am responsible for myself, you are responsible for yourself, and we all understand this is how the world works." When making decisions, the focus is often on "how does this affect me?" with an instinctive drive that everyone else is thinking the same way. Attention goes to issues of basic survival (food, shelter) and security (however security is defined for each type). People with this subtype are often quite aware of the physical aspects of their environment (temperature, space) and place an emphasis on ensuring security and physical needs are met.

Social
The social drive has an instinct of "The world functions better when we all get along." When making decisions, people with a social subtype tend to think holistically: "if I make this decision, how will it affect the group? If everyone in the group made this decision, what would that look like?" Attention goes to how one is positioned and regarded within groups. People with this subtype tend to have a keen awareness of group dynamics.

Intimate

The intimate drive has an instinct almost of "us against the world." The drive is to connect intensely with another person (this can be romantically, socially, professionally). This type is less interested in self-preservation and social dynamics and more focused on the intensity of individual connections. Attention goes to the quality and intensity of connection with certain individuals.

level 5:
SECURITY POINTS / STRESS POINTS

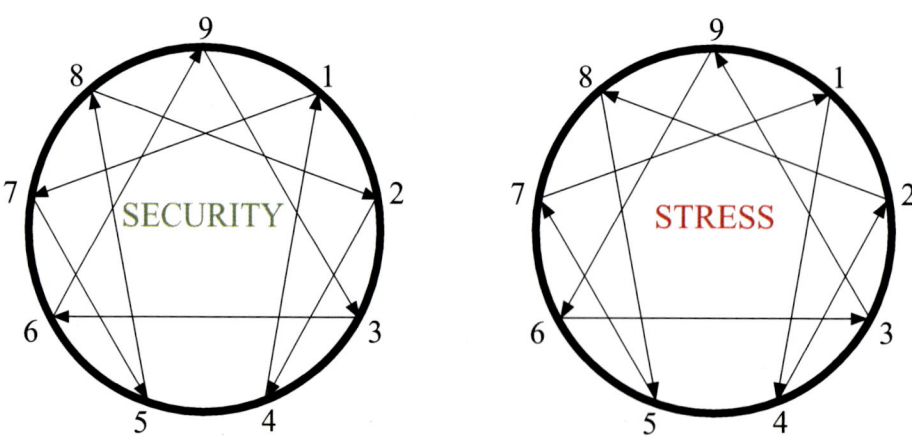

"When you are calm, quiet and sensitive then you can expand. But when you are irritated, phobic, fearful, insensitive and neurotic, you can't achieve anything."
~Yogi Bhajan

The stress and security points bring a fifth level of insight. The Enneagram recognizes that people behave differently in different environments, particularly when under stress and when feeling more relaxed and expansive. These differences are detailed through the system's use of security points and stress points.

Security points speak to how people behave when they are feeling relaxed and expansive. This is the behavior of someone who feels strong, confident and secure. While the basic psychological blueprint is still based on their primary type, the security point offers a path for personal growth and points to how a type behaves when the attention habit is relaxed. For each type, the growth path to relax the attention habit can be seen through the security point.

Stress points speak to the opposite, that is, how people behave when they are feeling stressed, tense and contracted. This is the behavior of someone who feels threatened, under pressure and insecure.

People can move from their stress point to security point within a single day or with much less frequency, depending on their external environment, the strength of their nervous system and their own personal emotional makeup and evolution. Both points help explain different behavior within each type.

The Map out of the Wilderness
The Enneagram provides a detailed map to explain human behavior—yours, and those around you. In the metaphor at the beginning of this guide book, the Enneagam serves as the map out of the wilderness. The next chapter describes Kundalini Yoga which gives you the resources you need to make the journey.

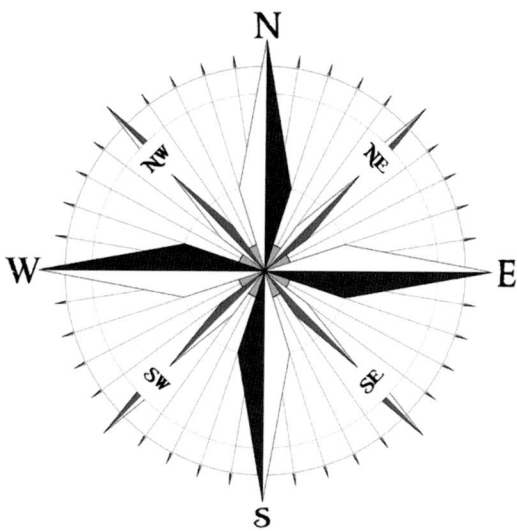

"You owe it to yourself to be yourself."
~Yogi Bhajan

KUNDALINI YOGA

 **Overview**

Kundalini Yoga is often referred to as the yoga of awareness. It combines physical exercises, breathing techniques, mantra, meditation and energy management into a single practice. The objective of Kundalini Yoga is to help people actualize their higher self and their life purpose. Long time practitioners often report, "Kundalini Yoga has helped me be more "me.""

The two main reasons I encourage people to try Kundalini Yoga are that it teaches you to control your mind, and it works quickly.

Yoga in its original form was a technology for enlightenment. A central goal of ancient yoga was to learn to control the mind. When yoga came to the West, many of the enlightenment and mind training pieces were deemphasized, and today's Western definition of yoga often focuses primarily on the physical exercises (asanas). While there is tremendous benefit in the asanas, it is only part of the story. Kundalini Yoga goes back to a more holistic yoga definition, training the mind as well as the body. A Kundalini Yoga practice typically ends with meditation, and the meditation is thought of as a very central part of the practice. The meditations typically include specific breathing techniques, and as I'll describe later, the key to controlling your thoughts is through your breath.

Kundalini Yoga also works very quickly. Most people feel uplifted, more relaxed and positive after a single session. Regular practice typically results in an increased sense of peace and happiness as well as increased clarity. And many people's lives have transformed completely after starting a regular Kundalini Yoga practice. That said, there are many forms of yoga and breathing techniques that are beneficial. Kundalini Yoga is merely one. It's the high speed jet to get to your destination. Some people don't want a high speed jet--they prefer a train, a car or to walk. It is important to find a practice that works for you.

Unlike many ancient religious philosophies, Kundalini Yoga does not hold onto any strict rules or dogmas. The pure nature of Kundalini Yoga has allowed each generation for thousands of years to find personal meaning in the practice. Kundalini Yoga does not claim to be the way to personal enlightenment and fulfillment; it is simply a way, one tool on each individual's journey to personal discovery.[4]

"Kundalini" is an ancient Sanskrit word that literally means "coiled snake." In early Eastern religion, it was believed that each individual possessed a divine energy at the base of the spine. This energy was thought to be the sacred energy of creation. It is something we are born with, but we must make an effort to "uncoil the snake" or release the energy thereby putting us in direct contact with the divine. Kundalini Yoga is the practice of awakening our Higher Self and turning potential energy into kinetic energy.[5]

The History of Kundalini Yoga[6]

The exact origin of Kundalini Yoga is unknown, but the earliest known mention dates to the sacred Vedic collection of writings known as the Upanishads (c. 1000 B.C. – 500 B.C.). Historical records indicate that Kundalini Yoga was a science of energy and spiritual philosophy before the physical practice was developed. The word "upanishads" literally translates to "sitting down to hear the teachings of the master." The first Kundalini Yoga classes were just that. Masters sat down with students and gave oral recitation of spiritual visions. This was a popular practice in ancient Vedic society (and would be replicated centuries later by Buddha and Jesus). Over time, the body science of Kundalini Yoga was developed as a physical expression of the Upanishad visions.

From its origin, Kundalini Yoga was not taught publicly. It was treated as an advanced education. Students were required to go through many years of initiation before they were prepared to learn the spirit-body lessons of the Kundalini masters. For thousands of years, the science of Kundalini Yoga was kept hidden, passed on in secret from master to a chosen disciple who was considered worthy. Teaching Kundalini Yoga outside the secret society of Indian yoga elite was unheard of. The public was not prepared, it was believed, to access such powerful knowledge.

This all changed in 1968 when a Sikh Master of Kundalini Yoga named Yogi Bhajan took a one-way flight from Punjab, India to Toronto, Canada.

[4-6] *Sat Nam: The Secret History of Kundalini Yoga by James McCrae*

Yogi Bhajan[7]

Yogi Bhajan (born Harbhajan Singh Puri) was born August 26, 1929, in the part of India that became Pakistan in 1948. He spent his youth in privileged environments in private schools and his summers in the exclusive Dalhousie mountain region of Himachal Pradesh. As a young boy he attended a Catholic convent school.

When he was eight years old he began his yogic training with an enlightened teacher, Sant Hazara Singh, who proclaimed Yogi Bhajan to be a Master of Kundalini Yoga when he was sixteen and a half.

During the turmoil of partition in 1947, at the age of 18, he led his village of 7,000 people, near what is Lahore Pakistan today, 325 miles on foot to safety in New Delhi, India, where he arrived with only the clothes on his back. Displaced Indians were given houses in India, and soon Yogi Bhajan was able to continue his education at Punjab University. He excelled in debate and was a star athlete, playing both hockey and soccer and earning the name "China wall" from his opponents.

After graduating with a degree in Economics, he began government service with India's Internal Revenue Department. He eventually moved to the Customs Service and become head of Customs at Palam International Airport (now known as New Delhi's Indira Gandhi Airport).[8] He married Inderjit Kaur in 1952. They had two sons, Ranbir Singh and Kulbir Singh, and a daughter, Kamaljit Kaur.

In September of 1968, Yogi Bhajan left India for Canada to teach yoga at Toronto University, carrying a letter of recommendation from Sir James George, Canadian High Commissioner in New Delhi, who had been his student. After two months in Canada, he flew to Los Angeles for a weekend visit. Arriving in Los Angeles virtually unknown, Yogi Bhajan met a number of young hippies, the spiritual seekers of that era, and immediately recognized that the experience of higher consciousness they were attempting to find through drugs, could be achieved by practicing the Science of Kundalini Yoga, while simultaneously rebuilding their nervous systems.

Breaking the centuries old tradition of secrecy surrounding the empowering science of Kundalini Yoga, Yogi Bhajan began teaching it publicly. With the yogic sciences of yoga, meditation, yogic philosophy and loving acceptance, he gave his students an effective alternative to the prevalent drug culture. He called it the "3HO" (healthy, happy, holy) way of life.

---

[7] *The Yogi Bhajan Library of Teachings, November 24, 1990*

From humble beginnings, teaching first at the East West Cultural Center and then in a student's furniture store in West Hollywood, "The Yogi" was like a magnet. Students flocked to his classes. Soon he was teaching at colleges and universities, including Claremont and UCLA and accepting invitations to teach in other cities.

In July of 1969 the non-profit 3HO Foundation (Healthy, Happy, Holy Organization) was incorporated in California.

From 1968 until his death in 2004, Yogi Bhajan taught over 8,000 Kundalini Yoga classes. He established the first teacher training program in 1969 and personally trained thousands of yogis and future teachers. Many Kundalini Yoga classes around the world today are taught by yogis who trained directly under him.[9]

Kundalini Yoga Classes

Kundalini Yoga classes follow a very specific format. Throughout the world, you can go to a Kundalini Yoga class and expect a very similar structure. This structure includes:

- Tuning in
- Warm up exercises (optional)
- Kriya
- Deep Relaxation
- Meditation
- Closing

1) Tuning in

We chant "Ong Namo, Guru Dev Namo" three times at the beginning of each Kundalini Yoga class. The mantra is in Gurmukhi, a language used in Punjab, India. Translated to English, the mantra means, "I bow to divine wisdom" or "I bow to the teacher within myself." The purpose of tuning in is threefold:

- It sets the intention that the class is beginning.
- Chanting this mantra has a specific physiological effect. It triggers the pituitary gland and changes the secretions of this gland in the endocrine system.
- It tunes you into the Golden Chain of teachers, an entire body of consciousness that guides and protects your practice.

Even when doing a Kundalini Yoga practice on your own, it is highly recommended you tune in using this mantra as you will get much more out of the practice.

---

[9] *Sat Nam: The Secret History of Kundalini Yoga by James McCrae*

2) Warm up exercises

Some classes will include warm up exercises. Others will go directly into the kriya. Warm up exercises are optional and usually include gentle exercises to work the spine, neck, arms and legs.

3) Kriya

A kriya is a series of physical exercises (including specified breath, mudras, etc.) designed for a specific effect. Kundalini Yoga literally has thousands of kriyas, and one of the benefits of the practice is you can find a kriya that aligns with your goals. There are kriyas for depression, anger management, the spine, the core, the liver and so on.. It is highly likely you can find a kriya that addresses your specific issue or goal. These kriyas should never be altered or modified. They have been passed down, in very specific and pure form, for thousands of years. The purity of Kundalini Yoga is one of its strengths.

4) Deep Relaxation

Deep relaxation is one of the most critical parts of a Kundalini Yoga practice. During relaxation, you rejuvenate your parasympathetic nervous system, distribute the energy you have built up during the kriya, help muscles release rigid patterning and adopt a more neutral state, promoting glandular shifts, centering yourself emotionally, releasing stress and assisting the body and mind in developing an understanding of its own 'natural state' so that it relaxes automatically throughout your day.[10]

> *"Deep relaxation is not just the absence of movement. It brings profound relaxation to the physical body, allowing us to enjoy and consciously integrate the mind-body changes which have been brought about during the practice of a kriya. We may sense the extension of the self through the magnetic field and the aura."*
> *~Yogi Bhajan*

To do deep relaxation, lie on your back with your arms at your side, palms facing up and relax completely. In a typical class, this relaxation lasts eleven minutes, but it can be shortened down to lower amounts of time as well.

5) Meditation

The meditation at the end of the Kundalini Yoga practice is really the heart of the practice. The meditations are as varied as the kriyas for various different effects and goals. Meditations generally include breathwork and may or may not include mantra.

---

[10] *All About Kundalini Yoga Relaxation by Ramdesh Kaur, Oct 29, 2012*

6) The Closing

"May the long time sun
Shine upon you,
All love surround you,
And the pure light within you
Guide your way on."

Each Kundalini Yoga class ends with two versus of "May the Long Time Sun Shine Upon You." This song has been the closing of Kundalini Yoga classes since the day in 1969 when Yogi Bhajan heard it being played by some of his students. He liked the song and decided to incorporate it into Kundalini Yoga classes as the closing.

Typically, the song is sung in two versus. When I teach a class, I ask my students to think of someone or something that needs their healing energy and to mentally send that out to them on the first verse. On the second verse, I ask them to shower themselves with that same healing energy.

To close the class after the song, we chant Sat Nam. Sat Nam is a phrase used commonly throughout Kundalini Yoga. Literally translated, Sat means truth and Nam means name. Loosely translated it can mean "truth is my name." It can also be a simple acknowledgement that the Great Mystery is who we are. As a greeting, saying Sat Nam is like saying "I see your true nature" or "I acknowledge the divine in you."

Two Key Concepts: The Breath and the Nervous System
Two of the most important concepts for any newcomer to Kundalini Yoga to understand are the breath and the nervous system. This powerful combination is what makes Kundalini Yoga remarkably effective as a tool for transformation.

The Breath

"When you are short of wisdom, breathe."
~ Guru Nanak

Most of us breathe between 16 to 20 breaths per minute as we go throughout our regular day. We're having a fairly rapid, fairly shallow breathing experience. As you become more trained, you can breathe as little as one to two breaths per minute. And when you slow your breathing down to four cycles or fewer per minute, you automatically change the way your brain processes information. You become calmer, less reactive and clearer and more positive in your thinking. At the same time, you take in more information.

The image of a horse, rider and chariot is a metaphor used often in describing the importance of the breath. Symbolically, the chariot represents your life, the horses represent your thoughts and the rider represents your soul (also referred to as your Higher Self). To live a more fulfilled life, you want the rider in control. But for most of us, the horses-your thoughts-are driving your life, pulling you every which way and generally running amok. To get the horses under control, you need to use reins. And symbolically, the reins represent your breath. If you can control your breath, you can control your mind. And if you can control your mind, you can hear the voice of your soul and live a more fulfilled life.

Kundalini Yoga focuses extensively on the breath. Almost all of the physical exercises have a synchronized breathing component. This breathing component is just as important as the physical exercises. This is a very key concept and helps explain why I say everyone who can breath can do Kundalini Yoga. The breathing techniques are the core of the practice, and this makes the practice accessible to people of all physical abilities.

For anyone new to Kundalini Yoga, it is helpful to remember the starting point is the breath. If you have any physical limitations that don't allow you to perform the full exercise, back up to the breath and visualize doing the physical motion. At a minimum, try to keep up with the breathing. There is tremendous power in your breath, and this practice really harnesses that power.

The Nervous System

> *"Stress is when an outside pressure is not matched and overcome by your inside intelligence."*
> -Yogi Bhajan

The nervous system is a combination of the brain, the spinal cord and the nerve endings throughout the body. You can think of the nervous system as a container. When your nervous system is weak, it is like having a thin paper cup as your container. Life events come in and quickly overflow the container, leaving you feeling overwhelmed, stressed and exhausted. When your nervous system is strong, it is like having a thick metal pot as your container. The same life events occur, but now your container has space for them so you feel stronger and more at ease. Having a strong nervous system makes you a happier, more relaxed person. And when the nervous system is developed enough to hold pain, you can heal.[11]

Kundalini Yoga is a practice specifically designed to strengthen the nervous system. This is one of the reasons it has different benefits than other forms of exercise (for example, running or working out at the gym). Many of the movements in Kundalini Yoga gently stretch the spinal cord and improve energy flow along the spine. Through synchronized breathing, Kundalini Yoga exercises also work to remove energetic imbalances in the body. When these imbalances are removed, energy flows more fully throughout the body, and old emotional and mental patterns can be dropped.

This is the magic of Kundalini Yoga and how it leads many people to personal transformation.

Kundalini Yoga Summary of Terms

Baby Pose
Come into Rock Pose and rest your forehead on the ground. Arms are alongside the body, palms facing up. This is a good posture for relaxation.

Bear Grip
Place the left palm facing out from the chest with the thumb down. Place the palm of the right hand facing the chest. Bring the fingers together. Curl the fingers of both hands so the hands form a fist. This mudra is used to stimulate the heart and to intensify concentration. It is more effective if the hands are pulled strongly.

Breath of Fire
Breath of fire is a rapid, rhythmic, continous breath through the nose. It is powered from the Navel Point and solar plexus. It is practiced through the nostrils with the mouth closed unless specifically stated otherwise. To exhale, the air is expelled powerfully through the nose by pressing the Navel Point and the solar plexus to the spine. To inhale, the upper

---

[11] *Kundalini Yoga for the Nervous System* by Nihal Singh, Jan 25, 2012

abdominal muscles relax, the diaphragm extends down, and the breath seems to come in as part of relaxation rather than through effort. The chest stays relaxed and slightly lifted through the breathing cycle. Breath of fire releases toxins and deposits from the lungs, mucous linings, blood vessel and other cells. It expands the lung capacity and increases vital strength.

Buddhi Mudra
To form Buddhi Mudra, touch the tip of the little (pinkie) finger and the tip of thumb together. The other three fingers are straight. This mudra creates capacity to clearly and intuitively communicate, and it stimulates psychic development.

Cobra Pose
Lie flat on the stomach and bring the hands under the shoulders, palms flat on the ground. Lift the chest and heart up first and let the head follow as you lean back. Straighten the arms. Ideally, keep your feet together. If you can't keep your feet together, keep your thighs together. If it is difficult to keep your arms straight, bend your elbows or bring your forearms to the ground.

Easy Pose
Sit and cross the legs comfortably at the ankles. Pull the spine up straight and press the lower spine slightly forward.

Ego Eradicator
Sit on the heels or in Easy Pose. Apply a jalandhara banda/neck lock. Lift the arms to a 60 degree angle. Then draw the shoulder blades down over the back of the ribs so the shoulders are away from the ears. Curl the fingertips into the pads of the palms at the base of the fingertips. Stretch the thumbs towards the sky. Close the eyes and begin Breath of fire. To end, touch the thumbs above the head and open the fingers.

Gyan Mudra
To form Gyan Mudra, the tip of the index finger touches the tip of the thumb. Other fingers are either straight (active position) or relaxed (passive position). This mudra stimulates knowledge, wisdom and the power to compute.

Jalandhara Banda (Neck Lock)
Sit comfortably with a straight spine. Lift the chest and sterum upwards. At the same time, gently stretch the back of the neck long and the chin towards the back of the neck. The head stays level and centered and does not tilt forward. The muscles of the neck and throat remain loose. Keep the face and brow relaxed. The stretch is automatically applied by the shift of relative position between the chin and chest. Do not force the head forward

or down. Among other things, Jalandhara Bandh seals in energy that is generated in the upper areas of the brain stem and makes it easier to focus on internal sensations and perceptions

Left Nostril Breathing
Close the right nostril using the thumb or index finger of the right hand. Inhale and exhale through the left nostril. The left nostril is associated with the ida naadi, and breathing through the left nostril is thought to be calming, cooling, relaxing and associated with lunar energy.

Long Deep Breathing
Inhale through the nose, expanding first the abdominal cavity, then the mid-chest area and finally the clavicle and upper chest in a smooth sequence. Exhale and empty the lungs in reverse of the inhale, first the clavicle and upper chest, then the mid-chest, and finally pulling in the abdominal muscles. This breath can be done lying on the back, or sitting in a chair or on the floor. Be sure to maintain a straight spine throughout. Long Deep Breathing is both calming and energizing, stimulates the glandular system and allows the lungs to work more efficiently by utilizing the lower lung area.

Mulbhand (Root Lock)
Mulbhand or Root Lock is a hydraulic lock at the base of the spine. It coordinates, stimulates and balances the energies involved in the rectum, sex organs and Navel Point. To apply Mulbhand/Root Lock, first contract the anal sphincter and feel the muscles lift upward and inward. Once these muscles are tightened, contract the area around the sex organ. This is experienced as a slight lift and rotation inward of the pubic bone. Then contract the lower abdominal muscles and the Navel Point towards the spine.

Pranayam
Pranayam is the science of breath and contolling the movement of prana through the use of breathing techniques.

Right Nostril Breathing
Close the left nostril using the thumb or index finger of the left hand. Inhale and exhale through the right nostril. The right nostril is associated with the pingala naadi, and breathing through the right nostril is thought to be energizing, warming, projective and associated with solar energy.

Rock Pose
Start by kneeling on both knees with the top of the feet on the ground. Sit with the heels under the sitting bones. The heels will press the two nerves that run into the lower center of each buttock. Keep the spine pulled straight.

Stretch pose
Lie on the back and push the base of the spine into the ground. Bring the feet together and raise the heels 6 inches/15 centimeters off the ground. Raise the head and shoulders 6 inches/15 centimeters off the ground. Stare at the toes with the arms stretched out pointing towards the toes. Palms should face down, and arms angle slightly out from the body.

Surya Mudra
Surya Mudra is formed by placing the tip of the ring finger (fourth finger) on the tip of the thumb. Practicing it gives revitalizing energy, nervous system strength, good health and the power to win.

Third Eye
The Third Eye is an energy center located at center of the forehead a little above the eyebrows. Mental focus at this location stimulates the pituitary gland and sushmuna (central nerve channel of the spine).

Venus Lock
To form Venus Lock, interlace fingers with left little finger on the bottom, with the right index finger on top for men and the left for women. The fleshy mounds at the base of the thumbs are pressed together. This mudra brings the ability to focus and concentrate.

Kundalini Yoga and the Enneagram Combined

"Share your strengths, not your weaknesses."
-Yogi Bhajan

In the following chapters I have combined Enneagram types with Kundalini Yoga kriyas and meditations. The goal of the Enneagram is to learn your attention bias so you can share your strengths and not your weaknesses. The goal of Kundalini Yoga is to strengthen your nervous system so you can relax your attention habit and let your strengths shine through.

While any Kundalini Yoga kriya or meditation can be used by a person of any Enneagram type, I have found that some Kundalini Yoga kriyas and meditations address more directly the growth path of specific Enneagram types. An overview of each Enneagram type is included along with a Kundalini Yoga kriya and mediation that goes well with each type. This interweaving of the two systems is based on my personal experience with my students and my personal knowledge of both systems.

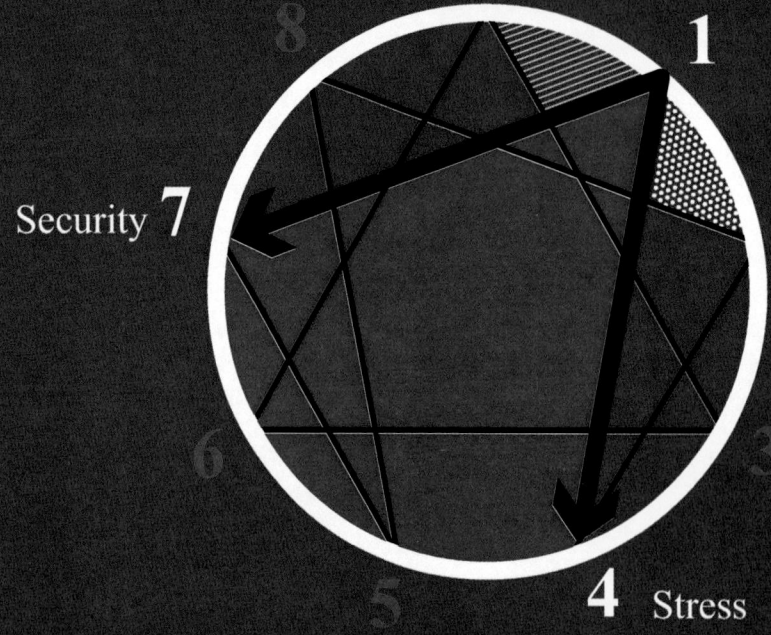

Enneagram Type One
THE REFORMER/ PERFECTIONIST

 ## Overview

Type One is called the Perfectionist or the Reformer because their attention automatically goes to what needs improvement and correction. They tend to see things in black and white, either perfect or imperfect, with very little gray in between. Type Ones feel pressure to be correct and to get things right. They have a tendency to analyze, and sometimes overanalyze, things. Type Ones have high standards and often find themselves in charge of projects or initiatives because they have a sense that "it will only be done right if I do it." They feel a great deal of personal responsibility for things they are involved in. Critical of others, they are even more critical of themselves.

 ## Type One Gifts to the World

Type Ones offer the world improvement either through increased efficiency, structure, planning and organization or in some instances, through moral heroism and radical social change. As their attention naturally goes to what can be improved, this action-oriented type moves to implement the improvements their minds naturally notice.

Type Ones Typically Report

1) A Desire to Get It Right
Type Ones report a desire to be perfect and to have a clear structure in which they can achieve perfection. This type often reports they can't really enjoy someting if they can't do it well. They seek a model to follow that clearly outlines the parameters to meet perfection.

> *"A friend invited us to dinner and asked us to arrive between 8:00 and 8:30. I almost didn't know how to interpret that. Internally I decided would arrive at 8:15. A range of time wasn't going to work for me at all."*

2) Extensive Social Contracts
A social contract refers to the idea that we all have unspoken social rules we understand and follow. For example, we inherently understand we don't throw trash on our neighbor's front lawn. We don't need to say it out loud—we all just understand it. Type Ones tend to have many more of these unspoken social contracts than the other types. As a classic example, Type Ones can become extremely irritated by people who park outside of the lines in a parking lot. They work hard to live up to high ideals, and they expect others to do the same.

> *"I've almost ended friendships over punctuality. It enraged me that one friend was constantly late. Then he finally let me know he didn't expect me to be on time for him, and suddenly, my anger vanished. But I almost ended the friendship before that point."*

3) They Become Exhausted by Their Own Thoughts and Efficiency
Most Type Ones report that it is exhausting to have the mind constantly correcting whatever they see and experience. Some report walking down the street can be irritating because they notice all the details that could be improved. Type Ones also sometimes report becoming exhausted by their own efficiency. Because they are natural and effective organizers, others often look to and lean on Type Ones to get things done. This responsibility can sometimes become disproportionate and draining.

> *"Sometimes I decide just to stay in the house all day because I know I'm going to get too irritated if I go out. I'll see all the things in the neighborhood that need correcting, and it annoys me so much I'd rather just stay home…"*

Tools for Compassion If You Have Type Ones in Your Life

1) Recognize they may be critical of you, but they are even harder on themselves

Type Ones can be critical, it is true, but they are even more critical of themselves. Most Type Ones report extreme self-criticism (often 10 on a scale of 1-10), and they criticize themselves "about everything--what I said, what I didn't say, what I ate for breakfast, what I did over the weekend." Keep this in mind the next time your Type One directs criticism your way.

2) Recognize that their constant correction isn't personal—it is just the way their mind works

Type Ones naturally see what needs correction—this is just what their minds do. As an action-oriented type, they also often proactively implement the changes they want. At a minimum, they might want to share with you what they notice. While it can feel personal, it isn't. Even when it is directed at you, it is just where their attention naturally goes. They can change their behavior and reaction to it, but this is the Type One experience and where the attention naturally gravitates.

3) Help them lighten up, laugh, have fun and slow down

Type Ones often feel the weight of the world on their shoulders. They can be efficiency machines, always thinking of the next thing that needs to be done and planning how to do it well. It can be very challenging for them to allow themselves time to relax and time for fun. Helping them laugh, lighten up, play and enjoy life is very healing for Type Ones.

 ## Next Steps If You are a Type One

1) The growth path for Type One is critical mind → curious mind → compassionate mind

As a Type One, notice when your mind automatically focuses on improvement which can manifest as criticism. Notice when you are reacting with criticism and try to open up space for curiosity. A good first step is to catch yourself starting to correct and instead insert the question—I wonder why it is that way? Allowing space for a question can help slow the automatic criticism/correction response.

2) Notice a tendency to feel everything falls on your shoulders or is your responsibility

As a Type One, you often feel like if you don't do it, it won't be done well enough. While there may be instances in which this is correct, this overall belief is a distortion and tires you out. Pick a small thing and delegate it. And then delegate another small thing and so on. Try to open your mind to the idea of "good enough."

3) If you notice an area in which you are particularly rigid (punctuality, organization, efficiency, neatness), try to be a little more relaxed
If you can't think of an area in which you are rigid, get candid feedback from your friends or family. A classic example is timeliness. If you notice you are extremely rigid or strict about timeliness, try to be five minutes late. Or if you are always thinking of the next thing that needs to be done, experiment with procrastinating and put something off. This will require nervous system work--and don't forget to breathe!

In the Body (The Energetics of Type One)

1) Type Ones tend to hold tension throughout their bodies in an attempt to repress emotion and specifically anger. Noticing and releasing building tension is important. A physical practice that helps move stuck energy and release tension is useful for Type Ones.

2) Type Ones can hold their bodies and faces rigidly. Consciously relaxing their facial muscles (a gentle smile) can be very beneficial.

3) Type Ones often have short, shallow breathing. Long deep breathing is a great practice to develop.

Take it a Step Further...

The Wings

1w9: The Idealist
Type Ones with a Nine wing are often more emotionally cool, understated in their presentation and a bit more philosophical in their approach to life than their Two wing counterparts. The Nine wing brings a calm, sometimes detached aura, and this type often operates more "behind the scenes."

1w2: The Advocate
Type Ones with a Two wing are more people-oriented and exhibit more interpersonal warmth than their Nine wing counterparts. The Two wing drives them to consider the human element in situations and can increase their feelings of empathy.

Stress and Security Points

Stress Point for Type One → Type Four, the Individualist/Artist/Romantic

When Type One is under stress, they go to Type Four, the Individualist/Artist/Romantic. This makes their behavior more emotionally driven, and they behave in a less organized, structured manner. The rational, principled typical behavior of Type One can become inconsistent and impulsive.

Security Point for Type One → Type Seven, the Enthusiast/Adventurer/Generalist

When Type One is feeling relaxed and expansive, they go to Type Seven, the Enthusiast/Adventurer/Generalist. This makes their behavior more playful and fun-loving, with less of an emphasis on getting it right and more of an emphasis on having fun in the moment. Many Type Ones report they feel this the most intensely when they are away on vacation, outside of their normal environment, when they don't feel the pressures of responsibility as acutely.

The Subtypes

Self-Preservation One: "Worry"

The self-preservation Type One expresses the drive to correct and improve by focusing that attention on his or her self. The attention goes to behaving well and correctly. To the outside world, this type is very warm, kind, tolerant and decent. Internally, this type is often very self-critical and filled with worry. This is a person who has a drive to control their environment, plan everything out and keep things under control. They have the title "Worry" because of a constant drive, expressed through worry, to achieve perfection, to avert misfortune or disaster and to avoid blame.

Social Type One: "Non-Adaptability"

The social Type One expresses the drive to correct and improve by focusing on his or her environment and striving to serve as a role model for others to follow. This is a person who wants to be a shining example of correct conduct and often expresses irritation that others don't act "as they should." To the outside world, this type can seem a bit detached, introverted or "above it all." Internally, this type feels a lot of irritation and typically doesn't feel totally comfortable in the groups they frequent. They have the title "Non-Adaptability" because of their predisposition to believe there is one right way to do things, and they know that way.

Intimate Type One: "Zeal"

The intimate Type One expresses the drive to correct and improve by focusing on intimate relationships and intimate partners. This is a person who has an intensity and drive to correct that is more exaggerated than in the other two subtypes. To the outside world, this type looks more like a reformer than a perfectionist. Internally, this type feels more direct anger than the other Type Ones and is driven to action with a sense of urgency. They have the title "Zeal" because of this intensity of desire and drive to correct.

The Kundalini Yoga Kriya and Meditation for Type One

"Let your heart speak to others' hearts."
~Yogi Bhajan

Kriya: For the Heart Connection
Meditation: To Burn Inner Anger

Because the growth path for Type One is from critical mind to curious mind and then compassionate mind, any physical or energetic work that connects them to their heart center is beneficial. Type Ones typically repress anger in an attempt to be "good." However, this repressed anger still builds energetically in the body, often causing health or emotional issues at some point in their lives. A growth opportunity for Type One can be to express or otherwise release this anger.

This Kundalini Yoga kriya is designed to cultivate the heart connection which in turn helps Type Ones access their compassionate mind.

The meditation is designed to burn out inner anger while strengthening the immune system.

Kundalini Yoga Kriya for Type One
Kriya for Heart Connection

Tune In:
Sit in Easy Pose with your legs crossed, bring your hands together in Prayer Pose at your heart center. Tune in and center yourself by chanting "Ong Namo, Guru Dev Namo" three times (see Tuning In on page 32).

Exercise 1:
Surya/Buddhi Mudra with Breath of Fire through the Mouth

Posture/Mudra	Breath	Full Time	1/3 Time
a. Right hand is in Surya Mudra (thumb touching fourth fingertip)	Breathe powerfully through "O" shaped mouth (with the power of navel point) so that the cheeks billow in and out. To End: Inhale deeply through the nose and hold for 30 seconds. Exhale and repeat twice.	3:30 minutes To End: Inhale and hold 30 seconds each time for three repetitions (1:30 minutes).	1:10 minutes To End: Inhale and hold 30 seconds.
b. Left hand in Buddhi Mudra (thumbtip touching pinkie fingertip)			
c. Bring the upper arms perpendicular to the ground with both hands up at sides of the head with palms facing forward.			

Exercise 2:
Hands to the Heart Center

Posture/Mudra	Breath	Full Time	1/3 Time
Place both hands over the heart. Focus eyes on the tip of the nose and meditate.	Let the breath find its own rhythm.	5:00 minutes	1:40 minutes
"Feel the goodness of the heart…Don't think of small things…think of oneness…"			

Exercise 3:
Knees to Chest and Jump Up and Down

Posture/Mudra	Breath	Full Time	1/3 Time
Pull knees up to the chest and lock them down tightly with the hands. Then jump up and down.	Let the breath find its own rhythm.	1:30 minutes	1:00 minute*

* time is not reduced to less than 1:00 minute

ENNEAGRAM TYPE ONE **THE REFORMER/PERFECTIONIST**

Exercise 4:
Lie on Back and Bring Arms and Legs to 90 Degrees with Breath of Fire

Posture/Mudra	Breath	Full Time	1/3 Time
Immediately lie on the back and raise legs and arms to 90 degrees, keeping the legs straight and pointing the toes. This exercise balances the meridians.	Heavy Breath of Fire	3:00 minutes	1:00 minute

Exercise 5:
Baby Pose

Posture/Mudra	Breath	Full Time	1/3 Time
Immediately come into Baby Pose (sitting on heels with forehead on the ground and arms beside the body) and go to sleep.	Let the breath find its own rhythm.	6:00 minutes	2:00 minutes

Exercise 6:
Lie on Back with Legs and Arms at 90 Degrees and Move Alternate Arms and Legs with Breath of Fire

Posture/Mudra	Breath	Full Time	1/3 Time
Immediately come into the same position as exercise #4, move arms and legs alternately back and forth.	Breath of Fire	2:30 minutes	1:00 minute*

*time is not reduced to less than one minute

ENNEAGRAM TYPE ONE **THE REFORMER/PERFECTIONIST**

Exercise 7:
Hands on Heart and Meditate

Posture/Mudra	Breath	Full Time	1/3 Time
Sit in Easy Pose, place hands on heart and meditate.	Let the breath find its own rhythm.	13 minutes	4:20 minutes
In the original class the students sang with Singh Kaur's Mender of Hearts, and the Gong was played the last 2:30 minutes.			
Total Kriya		36:00 minutes	12:40 minutes

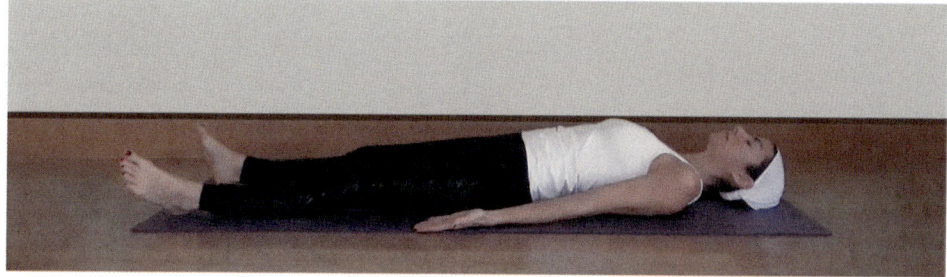

Deep Relaxation:
After you complete a Kundalini Yoga kriya, take a deep relaxation. This is when your body does its deep healing and incorporates some of the energy you have generated through the exercises. The relaxation can last anywhere from two to eleven minutes. To take a deep relaxation, lie on your back with your arms at your sides, palms facing up and relax completely.

HEADSTART FOR HAPPINESS

Kundalini Yoga Meditation For Type One
Meditation to Burn Inner Anger and Build the Immune System

Posture:
Sit in Easy Pose with a straight spine, chin in and chest out.

Mudra:
- Extend your index and middle fingers of your right hand and use the thumb to hold down the other fingers (your fingers are as if you are making a pledge).
- Raise your right arm in front of you and up to 60 degrees. Keep your elbow straight.
- Place your left hand over the heart center.

Eyes:
Eyes are closed.

Breath:
Make an "O" with your mouth and inhale and exhale powerfully through the mouth (2 second inhalation, 2 second exhalation) with strong, powerful breathing.

Mantra:
There is no mantra.

Time:
Start at 3 minutes per day and work up to 11 minutes a day.

To End:
- Inhale deeply and hold the breath for 10 seconds stretching both arms over head, and stretching the spine tall.
- Exhale powerfully like cannon fire through the mouth.
- Repeat this breath sequence 2 more times.

Comments from Yogi Bhajan:
"The breath should be strong and powerful and do it emotionally. Burn your inner anger, get rid of it...Take the help from the breath and get rid of the body's weakness and impurity."

Notes:
If you choose to practice this meditation for more than 40 days, switch the arm position after 40 days (i.e. raise the left arm, right hand over the heart center).

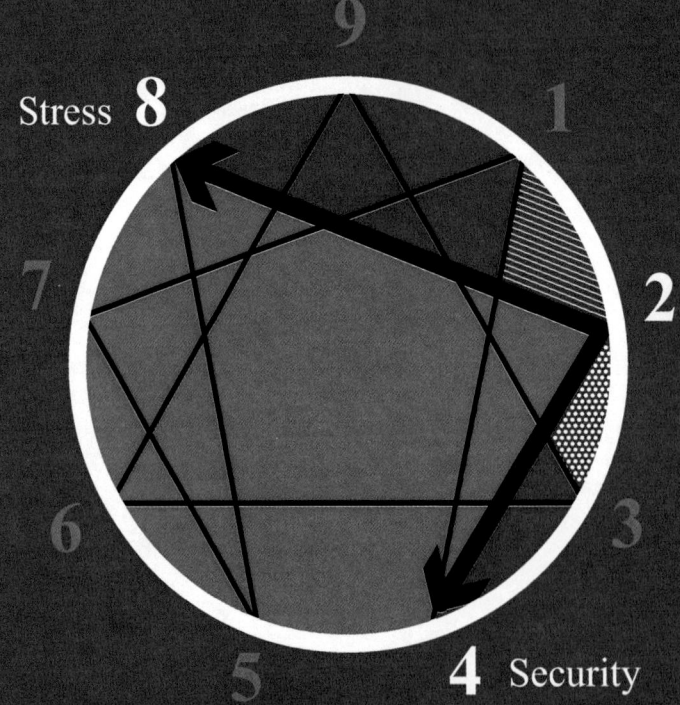

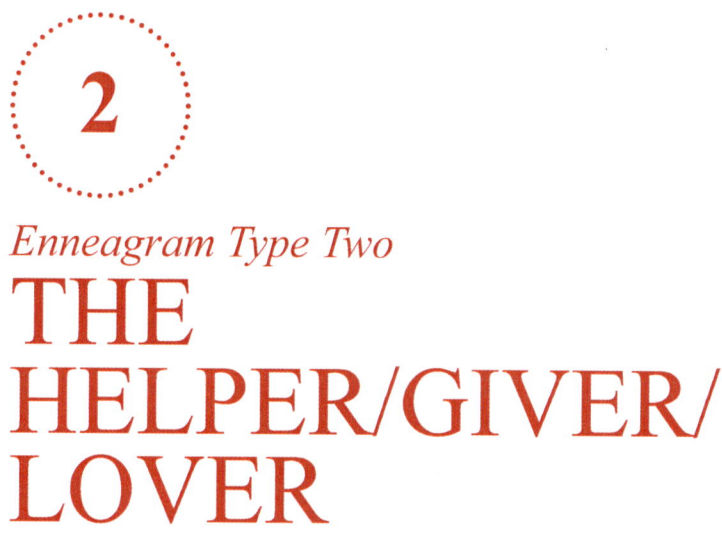

Enneagram Type Two

THE HELPER/GIVER/LOVER

Overview

Type Two is called the Helper, Giver or Lover because of their focus on being helpful, useful and likeable to other people. This is a very "other" referencing type whose attention easily and naturally goes out to other people. Type Twos often report having extreme sensitivity to the emotional state of the people around them, sometimes described as "an antennae I can't turn off." Type Twos often report being helpful to others as the meaning of life and typically struggle with boundary issues. It can be very hard for Type Twos to say no to a request someone makes of them, even if they really don't want to do it.

Type Two Gifts to the World

Type Twos can connect with others at a profoundly deep, heart-centered level. This type makes other people feel good, heard, understood, cared for, and through this connection, they can offer others deep healing. Gifted at reaching even the most emotionally distant, difficult people, Twos can reconnect others to the world.

Type Twos Typically Report

1) Offering Help Automatically

Type Twos often report that they offer help so automatically, they aren't even aware they are doing it. Just having another person physically present in the room changes the dynamic for a Type Two. Whenever someone else is present, their attention goes away from themselves and out to the others.

> *"Someone asked me once what I would do if I was in a room where no one needed anything. My mind almost can't imagine that. Everyone needs something—maybe they just haven't thought of it yet. So I would try to anticipate what people need…"*

2) Having Emotional or Physical Breakdowns because of Overextending Their Help

Type Twos often report having a complete physical or emotional breakdown at some point in their life as a result of helping others so much but not taking care of themselves. Type Twos are often in supportive roles in their jobs, communities, families and intimate relationships. They offer help to many while downplaying their own physical and emotional needs. A physical or emotional breakdown can be a big wake up call for a Type Two. While gifted at tuning into others, Type Twos can be surprisingly disconnected from their own needs.

> *"My wake up call was when I had a complete physical breakdown from being so overextended in my activities. I was volunteering three nights a week, helping my friends on the weekends, maintaining a full time job and trying to care for my own family. I knew I was tired, but it didn't occur to me that this was too much until my body just gave out. One day, I couldn't get out of bed I was so exhausted and that was pointing to a series of more serious health issues…."*

3) Having Unexpected Outbursts of Anger

Type Twos report having unexpected outbursts of anger. People of this type are usually very warm, caring and kind, but if they feel their efforts are not adequately recognized or appreciated they can become resentful and angry. If this resentment and anger persists in a repressed state, it can come out in unexpected explosions over seemingly small incidents. When the anger is unpackaged, it usually stems from a lack of appreciation for the Type Two's efforts or from a lack of gratitude.

> *"It took me a long time to understand how my helpfulness was linked to a desire for appreciation. But a lot of times, I would do something helpful for someone and imagine--fantasize really--about this really wonderful outcome. And if I didn't get that outcome, eventually I'd get angry."*

 ## Tools for Compassion If You Have Type Twos in Your Life

1) Recognize that it is very hard for them to say no to requests
While most of the other types don't suffer from personal boundary issues, Type Twos do. This makes it very difficult for them to say no to a request for assistance, even if it is inconvenient, impractical or to their own detriment. Type Twos often suffer from burnout trying to be helpful to everyone in their lives. Be mindful that if you ask a Type Two in your life to help you with something, it will be difficult for them to say no.

2) Tell the Type Twos in your life how much you appreciate them
Appreciation is like oxygen to them. It is particularly powerful if you tell Type Twos how much you appreciate them for them and not for their helpfulness. Type Twos can sometimes relax their compulsion to help if they feel appreciated for being themselves.

3) Realize that personal relationships are typically the most important thing in the life of a Type Two
Type Twos often define themselves by the relationships in their lives. Taking a little extra care cultivating your relationship with the Type Twos in your life can go a long way.

 ## Next Steps If You are a Type Two

1) Say no to a request for help or assistance
As a Type Two, you like to meet the needs of other people and maintaining personal boundaries can be difficult for you. A good first step is to gently but firmly say no to a request. This is usually uncomfortable and a bit anxiety provoking so starting small is a good idea. Learning to set boundaries and sticking to them is a crucial step in your personal growth. The ability to say no is an important part of this process.

2) Self-Nurture

Take some alone time each day to do something self-nurturing. For you to reach your highest level of functioning, you need to learn self-care. Carving out some time each day to cultivate this practice is important.

3) Take an honest inventory of the people with whom you have surrounded yourself

As a Type Two, you probably let many types of people into your life. It is often the emotionally draining ones who take up a large part of a Type Two's time. Seeking and cultivating equal, balanced relationships is important for you. Learn to be alert for a tendency to end up in one-sided relationships, where you are giving a lot and getting little in return. Allow others to be responsible for their own emotional state and calm your drive to change it for them.

In the Body (The Energetics of Type Two)

1) Type Twos have a tendency to energetically move outside of their own center of focus. When someone else enters a room, their attention automatically goes to that person. As a Type Two, when you notice this happening, you can come into balance by turning your attention to your breath and consciously sending energy down to your feet.

2) Type Twos have an easy time letting people into their lives but have a much more difficult time filtering them out. They have a tendency to let in too much. This is the same energetically where they can be out of balance between their prana and apana. Balancing the prana-apana (inhale, exhale) is important. Breathwork that focuses on this is beneficial.

3) Type Twos can get overly involved in the emotional state of others. As a Type Two, body work that grounds you and brings you back into your own body is really helpful. This can be dance, yoga, working out or any physical practice.

Take It a Step Further...

The Wings

2w1: The Servant

Type Twos with a One wing are typically more emotionally-contained, a bit more melancholy and quieter than their Three wing counterpart. The One wing brings a sense of ethics, respect and discretion.

2w3: The Host/Hostess
Type Twos with a Thee wing are more sociable and outwardly expressive with a stronger drive to get things done than their One wing counterpart. The Three wing can bring a level of image consciousness, style and often a flair for glamour.

Stress and Security Points

Stress Point for Type Two → Type Eight, the Leader/Challenger/Protector
When Type Two is under stress, they go to Type Eight, the Leader/Challenger/Protector. This makes their behavior much more direct, forceful and openly angry. It can also manifest in threats to withdraw from the relationship.

Security Point for Type Two → Type Four, the Individualist/Artist/Romantic
When Type Two is feeling relaxed and expansive, they go to Type Four, the Individualist/Artist/Romantic. This makes their behavior cover the full emotional spectrum regarding their own emotions—they are more likely to express sadness, pain, sorrow. Type Twos typically present a happy face because they inherently understand people like happy people. However, when they are feeling relaxed and expansive, they are more able to show others the fuller range of their emotions.

The Subtypes

Self-Preservation Two: "Privilege"
The self-preservation Type Two expresses the drive to be likeable more than the drive to be helpful and useful. To the outside world, this is a person who assumes a somewhat childlike appearance, and they can be less trusting and more reserved than the other two subtypes, adopting a sometimes helpless, me-first attitude. Internally, this type feels anxious about self-reliance and gravitates to situations where others will take care of them. They have the title "Privilege" because this type can be self-indulgent and hedonistic with an underlying unconscious belief that others must care for them.

Social Two: "Ambition"
The social Type Two expresses a drive to be helpful and useful in groups, companies and social settings. This is a person who is keenly aware of power and influence and naturally aligns to situations where he or she is influencing powerful people. To the outside world, this type can look like a leader and someone who is comfortable in the limelight. This is a more adult, "Power Two." Internally, this type is (either subconsciously or consciously) supporting others from a desire to gain loyalty and reciprocity. They have the title

"Ambition" because this type is highly driven towards success, competence and influence. This type is at its best at being a close advisor to the leader.

Intimate Two: "Aggressive/Seductive"

The intimate Type Two expresses a drive to be helpful, likeable and desirable to particular individuals. In an effort to establish power in the relationship, this is a person who is more driven to direct seduction and as such cultivates an attractive appearance. He or she can have an almost irresistible quality. To the outside world, this person is like the classic "femme fatale" (or homme fatale). Internally, this type feels he or she is seeking love and that search justifies all behavior. They tend to put a lot of energy and focus into relationships and can have a hard time letting go if the relationship doesn't work out. They have the title "Aggressive/Seductive" because this type actively pursues seduction of intimate partners or potential partners.

 ## The Kundalini Yoga Kriya and Meditation for Type Two

"You have to be you and that can only happen if you love yourself."
~Yogi Bhajan

Kriya: For Balancing Praana and Apaana
Meditation: For a Calm Heart

Type Twos focus on others and can get overinvolved in the lives and needs of the people around them. A growth opportunity for this type is to be still, to calm their emotions towards others and reconnect with themselves. Getting in touch with their own needs is a key growth step for Type Two.

This Kundalini Yoga kriya balances prana-apana (what we let in and what we expel). It also includes exercises to connect you with your body, including a full body scan.

The meditation is for a calm heart. In this meditation, the left palm is placed at the heart center, the natural home of prana. This creates a deep stillness in the heart. The right hand that throws you into action and analysis is placed in a receptive, relaxed mudra and put in the position of peace. This meditation slows the breath, bringing expansiveness and calmness, while still staying connected to the heart.

ENNEAGRAM TYPE TWO THE HELPER/GIVER/LOVER

Kundalini Yoga Kriya for Type Two
Kriya for Balancing Praana and Apaana

Tune In:
Sit in Easy Pose with your legs crossed, bring your hands together in Prayer Pose at your heart center. Tune in and center yourself by chanting "Ong Namo, Guru Dev Namo" three times (see Tuning In on page 32).

Exercise 1:
On Hands and Knees with Arm and Alternate Leg Extended Straight Out

Posture/Mudra	Breath	Full Time	1/2 Time
On your hands and knees raise the left leg up and the right arm straight forward. Hold the position. Change sides and repeat the exercise with the opposite arm and leg.	Let the breath find its own rhythm.	3:00 minutes on the first side, 2:30 minutes on the second side.	1:30 on the first side. 1:15 on the second side.

Exercise 2:
Back Bend from Navel Point Standing on Knees

Posture/Mudra	Breath	Full Time	1/2 Time
Stand on your knees, and put your arms straight over your head. Bend backward from the navel and move your arms in a circle; your upper shoulders move, but your knees do not move.	Let the breath find its own rhythm.	2:00 minutes	1:00 minute

ENNEAGRAM TYPE TWO **THE HELPER/GIVER/LOVER**

Exercise 3:
Front Life Nerve Stretch Grasping Soles of Feet

Posture/Mudra	Breath	Full Time	1/2 Time
Sit down and stretch your legs straight out. Grab the soles of your feet and bring your chin between your legs. Hold this position for 2:30 minutes. Then remain in the position and concentrate at your Third Eye for 2:30 minutes more. *In the original class, Yogi Bhajan played the gong for the last 2:30 minutes.	Let the breath find its own rhythm.	5:00 minutes	2:30 minutes

HEADSTART FOR HAPPINESS

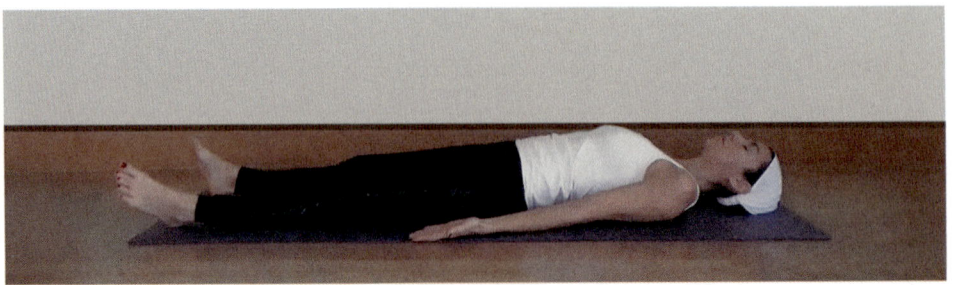

Exercise 4:
Corpse Pose/Body Scan

Posture/Mudra	Breath	Full Time	1/2 Time
Lie on your back and starting from your feet, move your attention up your body, deeply relaxing every part while you project your energy out of your Third Eye. *In the original class, Yogi Bhajan played the gong for the last 2:30 minutes.	Let the breath find its own rhythm.	6:00 minutes	3:00 minutes
Total time		18:30 minutes	9:15 minutes

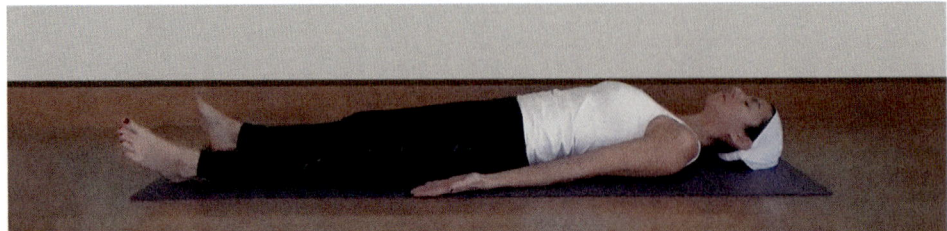

Deep Relaxation:
After you complete a Kundalini Yoga kriya, take a deep relaxation. This is when your body does its deep healing and incorporates some of the energy you have generated through the exercises. The relaxation can last anywhere from two to eleven minutes. **Because this Kundalini Yoga kriya includes a deep relaxation in the set, this second relaxation can be shortened so exercise four and the deep relaxation total eleven minutes.** To take a deep relaxation, lie on your back with your arms at your sides, palms facing up and relax completely.

ENNEAGRAM TYPE TWO THE HELPER/GIVER/LOVER

Kundalini Yoga for Type Two
Meditation for a Calm Heart

Posture:
Sit in Easy Pose or in a chair with a straight spine and a light neck lock.

Mudra:
Left hand:
Place the left hand on the center of the chest at the Heart Center. The palm is flat against the chest, and the fingers are parallel to the ground, pointing to the right.

Right hand:
Bring the right hand into Gyan Mudra (right thumb tip and tip of the index finger touch). Raise the right hand up as if giving a pledge. The right elbow is relaxed and to the side with the forearm perpendicular to the ground. The right palm faces forward. The 3 fingers not in Gyan Mudra (the middle, fourth, and pinky fingers) point straight up.

Eyes:
The eyes are either a) closed or b) look straight ahead with the eyes 1/10 open.

Breath:
Concentrate on the flow of the breath. Regulate each bit of the breath consciously. Inhale slowly and deeply through both nostrils. Then suspend the breath in and raise the chest. Retain (hold) the breath as long as possible. Then exhale smoothly, gradually and completely. When the breath is out, lock (or hold) the breath out as long as possible.

Mantra:
There is no mantra.

Time:
Start at 3 minutes, work up to 31 minutes.

To End:
Inhale and exhale strongly 3 times. Relax.

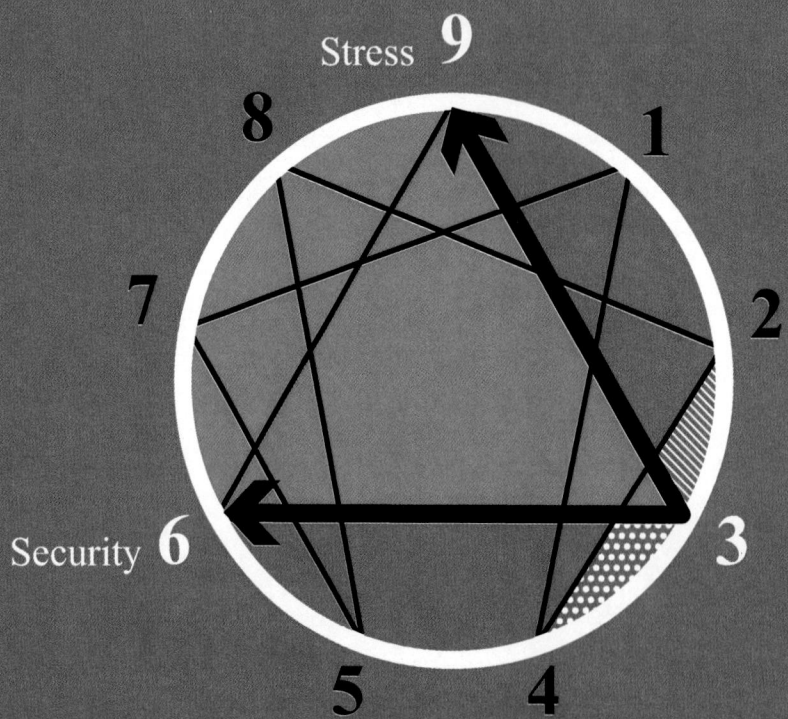

Enneagram Type Three
THE ACHIEVER/ MOTIVATOR

Overview

Type Three is called the Achiever or Motivator because their attention goes out to success and achievement. They have an innate ability to motivate others. This type is a very action-oriented, often successful person who naturally presents a positive image to the outside world. Gaining the admiration of others is important to them, and they put a lot of energy into the achievement of their goals. Type Threes typically align around "roles" (predefined ways of being) and focus on being successful in that role. In this way, Type Threes can sometimes confuse themselves for other types. However, they usually recognize their Type Three identity when they uncover that their primary motivation is to be the best. A classic example is a nun who looks like a Type Two Helper but who eventually realizes she actually wants to be recognized as the best nun more than she wants to helpful.

Type Three Gifts to the World

Type Threes are gifted leaders and motivators. Highly inspirational and often charismatic, they can naturally organize and energize groups. Goal-oriented and highly effective, they can successfully achieve their targets. The supreme motivators of the Enneagram, Type Threes help others reach their full potential.

Type Threes Typically Report

1) A Desire to be the Best in Every Situation
Type Three attention goes to success and wanting to be recognized as the best in almost all situations. They generally don't like doing things they aren't good at, and they are typically competitive, even in environments where it doesn't make sense.

> *"I knew I was a Type Three when I attended a neighbor's party. I'm a white guy living in a largely Hispanic neighborhood, and this was a Mexican party. I walked in the door, and my mind immediately went to how I could be the best Mexican at this party. And I'm a white guy—I'm not going to win that contest. But it was in my mind..."*

2) Packaging Up Inconvenient Feelings and Emotions and Putting Them Aside to Deal with Later
Type Threes are efficiency machines and very action-oriented. They often report impatience with others who are slowing down their achievement. In the same manner, emotions can slow them down. They often suppress their emotions as they see them as weaknesses. Type Threes may report going through very emotionally difficult times but freezing the emotions out and "putting them in a box to deal with later." To the rest of the world this can look cold or shut down, but for Type Threes, it is coping mechanism to allow them to continue on their achievement quest.

> *"It's not my favorite thing about myself, but it is true. If something becomes too intense, I just shut down around it—put the feelings in a box, and we'll deal with that later..."*

3) Public Admiration and Praise is Important to Them
While not all Type Threes readily admit it, most will privately say that public admiration and praise is quite important to them. Their main motivator is popular acceptance and recognition. Type Threes feel their identity from the outside in, so having a strong internal compass free from external influence is difficult for them.

> *"I use public praise as a marker for how I'm doing. Without external approval, I really don't know...."*

Tools for Compassion If You Have Type Threes in Your Life

1) Tell them what you like about their character and don't focus on their achievements
Type Threes over identify with their achievements and activities and under identify with their character and emotional makeup. Telling them what you like about their behavior and character can be very eye-opening and healing for them.

2) Give them honest but not overly critical feedback
No one likes criticism, but Type Threes almost can't bear to hear it. If you have negative feedback to give to a Type Three, make sure to deliver it in a balanced, constructive way. This is a type who does learn from criticism, but too much negative criticism will be blocked completely.

3) Be aware they don't like to dwell in negative emotions or situations where they might fail
Type Threes like to focus on their successes and on positive emotions. They gravitate away from areas in which they are likely to feel negative emotions and towards areas in which they'll get positive feedback. Type Threes sometimes avoid or drop relationships entirely if the situation becomes too negative or difficult.

Next Steps If You are a Type Three

1) Notice a tendency towards workaholism and keeping yourself busy with activities
As a Type Three, you love to achieve—it energizes you. However, this may be blocking your ability to feel and process your emotions. Try to build in some time each day to slow down and allow your emotions to rise. Kundalini Yoga breathing exercises are a great starting practice for this.

2) Cultivate personal creativity in an environment with no audience
It is important to learn to be alone, where there is no public admiration, no applause, no recognition, no external feedback loop. In this space, your true creativity can arise.

3) Share a vulnerability with someone close to you
Type Threes often report difficulty with intimacy in their relationships. The drive to present themselves as a success can cut Type Threes off from genuine connection with

others. Sharing a vulnerability with someone close to you can be a great first step in developing more intimate, authentic relationships.

In the Body (The Energetics of Type Three)

1) Type Threes have a drive to rush forward into action that can result in a denial of feelings. Slowing down helps Type Threes experience their emotions more fully.

2) Impatience towards others is a trademark characteristic of Type Threes. This impatience feels like a rush of energy and contraction in the body and breath. When impatience starts to develop, it is helpful to breathe deeply from the belly. This automatically works to relax the body and calm the mind.

3) The Type Three energy goes out to notice what other people are thinking of them. Any practice done with the eyes closed is really helpful for Type Threes as it forces them to tune in more fully to their own body and experience.

Take It a Step Further...

The Wings

3w2: The Charmer
Type Threes with a Two wing are typically more social, warm, extroverted and openly seeking approval than their Four wing counterpart. The Two wing brings a people-pleasing element, a focus on others and a more emotionally expressive presentation.

3w4: The Professional
Type Threes with a Four wing are more introverted, focused on their creative expression and internally competitive with themselves than their Two wing counterpart. The Four wing can bring a level of creativity and familiarity with the darker emotions (sadness, melancholy).

Stress and Security Points

Stress Point for Type Three → Type 9, the Peacemaker/Mediator
When Type Three is under stress, they go to Type Nine, the Peacemaker/Mediator. This makes their behavior more sloth-like, slow moving, unenergized and can even become full-blown depression. The normally energetic Type Three can have a hard time motivating to get things done.

Security Point for Type Three → Type Six, the Loyalist/Doubter/Skeptic
When Type Three is feeling relaxed and expansive, they go to Type Six, the Loyalist/Doubter/Skeptic. This makes their behavior more team-oriented and collaborative. The normally competitive Type Three starts to care more about the state of the group or team and can slow down their pace.

The Subtypes

Self-Preservation Type Three: "Security"
The self-preservation Type Three expresses a focus on achievement and a drive to succeed in an understated, humble way. This is a type that considers it bad manners to openly brag about his or her accomplishments, although most self-preservation Type Threes privately admit they do enjoy public praise and admiration. To the outside world, this type seems like a hard-working, successful, humble person who excels professionally in his or her chosen field. This is a person who goes beyond wanting the image of success. It is important to them that they actually are good in their respective fields and roles. Internally, this person is often experiencing a great deal of anxiety. They address this anxiety by working harder in an attempt to achieve more security. They have the title "Security" because of their preoccupation with work, efficiency and security.

Social Type Three: "Prestige"
The social Type Three is often who we think of when we hear Type Three. This type expresses a focus on achievement by outwardly seeking admiration and highlighting his or her achievements and successes. This person can be a social chameleon, shape shifting to shine as much as possible in whatever environment he or she is in. To the outside world, this can look like someone who is socially brilliant. They can usually adapt in various social situations with people with different backgrounds. They want to be accepted so feeling sociable with others is critical. The social Type Three is generally comfortable in the spotlight and likes the attention of others. This is the most externally competitive of the Type Threes. Internally, this type has a lot of anxiety about being overexposed, and criticism can be devastating to them. They sometimes express a fear that if they look too deep inside, they will find there is nothing there. This type is titled "Prestige" because of their desire to have the approval and applause of others.

Intimate Type Three: "Charisma"
The intimate Type Three expresses a drive for achievement and recognition through intimate relationships. This is a person that focuses energy on being attractive and desirable. More shy, sweet and reserved than the other Type Threes, this person can be uncomfortable with direct recognition and instead focuses his or her energy on promoting someone

or something else. To the outside world, this is an attractive, sometime seductive person who often offers enthusiastic support to others. They are highly helpful and supportive, often striving to be the perfect role model (for example, the perfect husband or wife). Internally, this person often feels a deep sadness or emptiness and sometimes fantasizes about a perfect mate and a happy future. This type is titled "Charisma" because of their intense focus on desirability and attracting the devotion of others.

The Kundalini Yoga Kriya and Meditation for Type Three

"You cannot make your life a reaction to others;
you must make your life your own."
~Yogi Bhajan

Kriya: Balancing the Head and Heart
Meditation: To Change the Ego

While Type Three is in the Heart/Feeling center, this type is often cut off from their heart and their emotions. A growth step for Type Three is to reconnect with their heart, to place less importance on what others think of them and to learn the value of their own emotional world.

This Kundalini Yoga kriya helps to bring a balance between logic and feeling and between an overly intellectual mind and overly sensitive emotions. Energetically, it aligns the head and heart so you can be great and graceful, aware and loving. Physically, the exercises change the chemistry of the brain fluid and open the lower back and hips.

This meditation is designed to change the ego making it easier for the true self, the soul, to come forward.

Kundalini Yoga Kriya for Type Three
Balancing the Head and the Heart

Tune In:
Sit in Easy Pose with your legs crossed and bring your hands together in Prayer Pose at your heart center. Tune in and center yourself by chanting "Ong Namo, Guru Dev Namo" three times (see Tuning In on page 32).

PART ONE:
INHALE AS FINGERS POINT UP

PART TWO:
EXHALE AS FINGERS POINT FORWARD

PART THREE:
INHALE AS FINGERS POINT UP

PART FOUR:
EXHALE AS FINGERS POINT BACK

Exercise 1:
Arms Out Parallel to Ground, Hands Rotate in Rhythm

Posture/Mudra	Breath	Full Time	1/3 Time
In Easy Pose with the arms outstretched, hands bent at the wrists at a 90 degree angle. This exercise has a four part sequence:	Inhale up (first and third positions). Exhale forward and backward (second and fourth positions). One cycle should take approximately 4 seconds.	6:00 minutes	2:00 minutes
a. fingers together pointing up, palms facing out			
b. rotate hands so fingers point straight forward			
c. return to original position with fingers pointing up			
d. rotate hands so fingers point straight back			

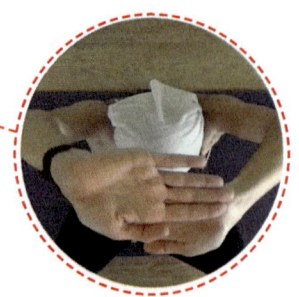

PART ONE:
INHALE ARMS OVERHEAD AS HANDS CROSS IN FRONT

PART TWO:
EXHALE AS ARMS EXTEND OUT PARALLEL TO THE GROUND

PART THREE:
INHALE ARMS OVERHEAD AS HANDS CROSS IN BACK

Exercise 2:
Arc Hands Over Head

Posture/Mudra	Breath	Full Time	1/3 Time
This exercise has a three part sequence. Stay sitting in Easy Pose, arms straight out to the sides parallel to the ground, with palms out.	Inhale and raise the arms up to form an arc. Exhale and lower the arms straight out to the sides once more.	1:00-2:00 minutes	1:00 minute*
a. Inhale and raise arms in an arch, palms crossing each other slightly in front of the top of the head, without touching each other.			
b. Return arms to the outstretched position on the exhale.			
c. Inhale and arch arms overhead, palms up as before, but slightly behind the top of the head.			

* time is not reduced to less than 1:00 minute

PART ONE:
EXHALE ARMS STRAIGHT OUT IN CROW POSE

PART TWO:
INHALE TO STANDING WITH HANDS CROSSED ABOVE HEAD

Exercise 3:
Crow Pose with Arms Parallel to Ground to Standing with Arms Crossing above Head

Posture/Mudra	Breath	Full Time	1/3 Time
Continue the arm movement of exercise #2 and add crow squats. As you exhale, squat down in crow pose with arms out to the side. As you inhale, stand up with arms overhead.	Inhale up, exhale down.	3:00-4:00 minutes with a rhythm of one second per movement	1:00-1:20 minutes
Total Time		10:00 to 12:00 minutes	4:00 to 4:20 minutes

Deep Relaxation:
After you complete a Kundalini Yoga kriya, take a deep relaxation. This is when your body does its deep healing and incorporates some of the energy you have generated through the exercises. The relaxation can last anywhere from two to eleven minutes. To take a deep relaxation, lie on your back with your arms at your sides, palms facing up and relax completely.

ENNEAGRAM TYPE THREE **THE ACHIEVER/MOTIVATOR**

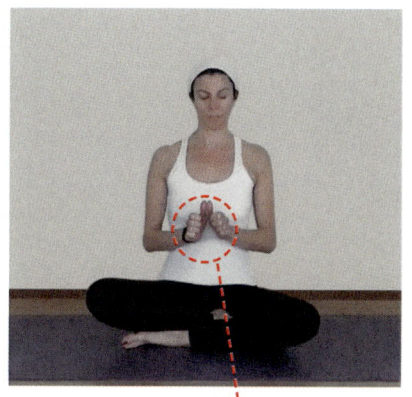

Kundalini Yoga Meditation for Type Three
Meditation to Change the Ego

Posture:
Sit in Easy Pose or in a chair with a straight spine and a light neck lock. Keep the spine straight and the chest slightly lifted.

Mudra:
Raise the hands in front of the center of the chest at the level of the heart. The palms face each other. Curl the fingers into a loose fist. Keep the thumbs extended and point them upwards. Bring the hands towards each other until the top segment of the thumbs touch along the side of the thumbs. The rest of the hands stay separated. The arms are relaxed and to the side.

Eyes:
Fix the eyes on the knuckles of the thumbs. Narrow the eyelids.

Breath:
Bring your concentration to the breath. Create a steady breath rhythm with the following ratio and flow:

a) Inhale slowly through the nose. The length is approximately 8 seconds.

b) Hold the breath for approximately 8 seconds.

c) Exhale the breath through the nose in 8 equal strokes.

d) Hold the breath out for 8 seconds.

Once this pattern is set, you can increase the length as long as you like. If you increase the time, keep the time equal in each section of the pranayam.

Mantra:
There is no mantra.

Time:
Start at 3 minutes, work up to 31 minutes.

To End:
Inhale deeply, stretch the hands over the head, and open and close the fists several times. Relax the breath.

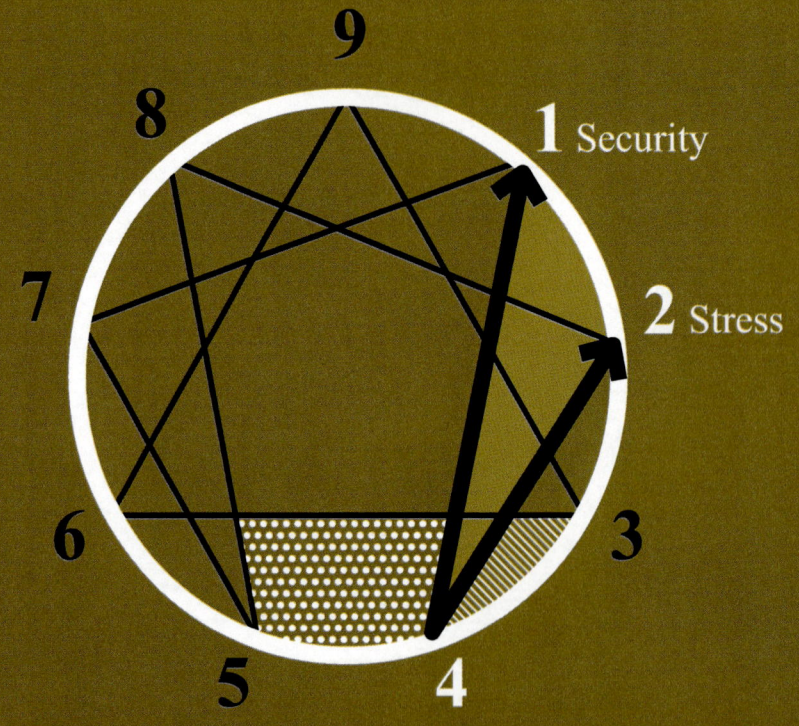

Enneagram Type Four
THE INDIVIDUALIST/ ARTIST/ ROMANTIC

 **Overview**

Type Four is called the Individualist, the Artist and the Romantic because of their focus on individuality, authenticity and full expression of their emotions. This type owns the emotional spectrum—they've been up, they've been down, they've been everywhere in between and often are on a regular basis. Type Fours experience the world with great emotional intensity, and their attention naturally goes to what is missing in their lives. They are very committed to authenticity and are comfortable operating far outside of the range of mainstream taste. Strong emotions serve as a guide for what is important.

 Type Four Gifts to the World

Profoundly committed to authenticity and willing to operate outside of the mainstream, Type Fours offer the world ingenuity, inspiration and originality. They can access profound creativity and offer the world inspired creations. Because they feel so intensely, they can channel this intense emotion into creative works that impact others profoundly. In addition, because of their mastery of the emotional spectrum, Type Fours teach the rest of us how to feel more and how to access a fuller range of emotion. No emotion scares them, and this fearlessness can be deeply healing for the rest of us.

Type Fours Typically Report

1) Extreme Emotional Sensitivity and a Preference to Intense Emotions over Flat, Moderate Emotions

Type Fours really do feel more than most of the other types. They can access more of the emotional spectrum and spend more time focusing on and processing their feelings.

> *"They say that Eskimos have about 50 words for "snow" because as an Eskimo, a lot of your life revolves around the snow. I have this same experience for the emotional world. I have 50 words for sadness. I spend a lot of time feeling my emotions and processing exactly what I'm feeling."*

Type Fours also typically report they prefer having big emotional ups and downs over having a "regular day." They like the emotional intensity, even though they report it can be extremely exhausting. For Type Fours, the emotional spikes are often what make life worth living.

> *"I would take a good, deep, dark depression over a regular day anytime."*

2) They Struggle with Their Identity

Type Fours often struggle with wanting a stable sense of their own identity and their everchanging emotions. Authenticity is a core value for Type Fours, and since they use their emotions as a guide, it feels inauthentic to downplay their emotional world. But this emotional world can also feel unstable, so they often are torn between over identifying with their emotions and seeking something more stable to use as a foundation for their identity. Most Type Fours report they struggle to establish a clear and authentic identity.

> *"I had been thinking about changing my name for a few years - not because I hated my birth name, but because I wanted a name that communicated something true and deep about my inner life. Naming myself was an act of integration and authenticity: a way to reclaim power over my life, to stand inside my experience and say, "This is who I am in the world.""*

3) Chronically Undervaluing Themselves

Type Fours chronically undervalue themselves and their achievements. While they are often very accomplished in their respective fields, they don't recognize this as their attention naturally goes to what is missing in their lives. This can manifest as low self-esteem or an internal conflict between feeling inferior and at the same time feeling superior.

> *"It isn't exactly a "grass is always greener" feeling. It feels more like, well, if I could do it, it must not be very hard…"*

 ## Tools for Compassion If You Have Type Fours in Your Life

1) Don't tell them they are too sensitive or dramatic
Type Fours experience the world very intensely. This is their experience. Telling them not to be so sensitive or dramatic isn't helpful. They aren't choosing to experience life the way they do—it is how their brains are wired.

2) Be supportive and use humor to lighten up a situation
Type Fours assign disproportionate importance to their emotional world so helping them to lighten up with humor and support goes a long way. Type Fours can get a lot of benefit from others who hold the space for their emotions but don't get caught up in the drama of them. A good dose of lightness and humor can diffuse some of the intensity.

3) Recognize that geniune compliments mean a lot
Type Fours undervalue themselves so getting positive feedback regularly can be really healing for them. However, make sure the compliments are genuine. Type Fours are very sensitive to anything that feels inauthentic to them so a disingenuous compliment can do more harm than good.

 ## Next Steps If You are a Type Four

1) Set up positive daily routines and create small, realistic goals that you can work towards achieving
As a Type Four, you tend to get swept into the intensity of your emotional world. This can pull you off center and make you feel unstable. Try to set up positive daily or weekly routines. This can provide a stablizing framework when your emotions begin to change. As a Type Four, you can sometimes get lost in a fantasy future or have unrealistically high expectations for your short-term goals. Small, realistic, achievable goals can help keep you on track.

2) Notice when you start to withdraw if you want attention or if your feelings have been bruised. Consider other reactions
The tendency to withdraw for attention can be a subconscious one so it is sometimes hard to recognize. When you do recognize that you've withdrawn, it is important to understand that other people aren't mind readers and don't realize you are trying to make a point. Instead, they are often left confused. Consider more direct approaches to get your needs met.

3) Use your deep well of creativity and self-expression as an outlet for your shifting emotions and changing identity
One of your strengths is your creativity and your self-expression. Use these strengths to channel your ever-shifting emotions into something powerfully creative. Channeling your emotional swings into something constructive will help stabilize you and give you a clearer sense of yourself.

In the Body (The Energetics of Type Four)

1) Type Fours tend to be very sensitive and often take in quite a bit from their external environment. A strong nervous system and strong aura are important for Type Fours.

2) Emotions rule the world of Type Four so noticing the energy of emotions is important. Emotions can center in a particular part of the body so getting the energy moving and circulating all throughout the body is helpful. Walking meditations can be particularly beneficial for Type Fours as the entire body is automatically engaged.

3) Type Fours have a tendency to withdraw for attention. This withdrawal can be emotional, physical or energetic. Notice when your body contracts. As you start to contract and withdraw, consciously try to relax your body.

Take It a Step Further...

The Wings

4w3: The Aristocrat
Type Fours with a Three wing are typically more practical, image conscious and in some instances glamorous than their Five wing counterparts. The Three wing can bring social or business savvy making them successful in the material world.

4w5: The Bohemian
Type Fours with a Five wing are typically more isolated, intellectual and idiosyncratic than their Three wing counterpart. The Five wing brings a complexity and search for meaning on multiple levels.

Stress and Security Points

Stress Point for Type Four → Type Two, the Helper/Giver/Lover
When Type Four is under stress, they go to Type Two, the Helper/Giver/Lover. This makes their behavior more over involved in the lives of others, and they can appear clingy. Their tendency to withdraw drops, and they can seem needy.

Security Point for Type Four → Type One, the Perfectionist/Reformer
When Type Four is feeling more secure and expansive, they go to Type One, the Perfectionist/Reformer. This makes their behavior more objective, rational and principled. They are influenced less by the emotional world, and while they still feel their intense range of emotions, they "buy into the story" less. During these periods, they tend to be highly productive.

The Subtypes

Self-preservation Type Four: "Tenacity"
The self-preservation Type Four expresses the emotional intensity of the type more stoically than the other subtypes. This is a person who suffers in silence and is sometimes referred to as the "Sunny" Four. To the outside world, this person can seem reserved and introspective. Internally, this type is often feeling a wide range of intense emotions on a regular basis. However, this intensity is often not expressed to others. They have the title "Tenacity" because of their tendency to hold it all together, to suffer in silence.

Social Type Four: "Shame"
The social Type Four openly expresses the emotional intensity of the type, feels things deeply and presents the sense of shame closer to the surface than the other subtypes. This is sometimes called the "Sad" Four. To the outside world, this is someone who communicates suffering openly and regularly. Others may see this person as dramatic and overly emotional. Internally, this is a person who feels a lot of suffering and whose attention goes naturally to his or her own deficiencies. They have the title "Shame" because this type openly experiences and identifies with shame more than the other subtypes.

Intimate Type Four: "Competition"

The intimate Type Four expresses emotional intensity and envy through competition and an attempt to establish superiority. This type is characterized as the angriest type in the Enneagram, and this person typically has a colorful, vivid personality. It is hard to forget an intimate Type Four. This type is sometimes called the "Mad" Four. To the outside world, they appear intense, opinionated, strong-willed and sometimes angry. Internally, this person is feeling misunderstood, competitive and a mix of inferiority and arrogance. Conversely, this type can also express great sensitivity, understanding and tenderness. This person is a study in contrasts. They have the title "Competition" because of their keen focus on competition and being the best.

The Kundalini Yoga Kriya and Meditation for Type Four

"The moment you value yourself, the whole world values you."
~Yogi Bhajan

Kriya: To Strengthen the Aura
Meditation: Inner Conflict Resolver Reflex

Type Fours are usually very sensitive and can struggle with their intense and ever-changing emotions. A growth opportunity for Type Four is to learn to stay relaxed in the face of intense emotions and to remain neutral, even when feeling big emotional swings.

This Kundalini Yoga kriya builds and strengthens the aura, the energetic field that surrounds us. When your aura is strong, external influences will have less of a negative impact on you, and you feel more stable and secure. Feeling stable and secure is good for all types, but particularly Type Four, who experiences a lot of inner turmoil.

The meditation Inner Conflict Resolver Reflex helps cultivate stability. Type Fours can place an over-importance on their emotional state and are sometimes left feeling unstable and conflicted. Confusion and inner deadlock can block their ability to think and act clearly. This meditation is a wonderful stabilizer by controlling the breath while staying connected to the heart center.

Kundalini Yoga Kriya for Type Four
Kriya for Strengthening the Aura

Tune In:
Sit in Easy Pose with your legs crossed, bring your hands together in Prayer Pose at your heart center. Tune in and center yourself by chanting "Ong Namo, Guru Dev Namo" three times (see Tuning In on page 32).

INHALE

EXHALE

Exercise 1:
Triangle Push Ups

Posture/Mudra	Breath	Full Time	1/3 Time
Stand up and bend forward so the palms are on the ground and the body forms a triangle. Raise the right leg up with the knee straight. Continue and then change legs.	Exhale, bend the arms and bring the head near the ground. Inhale, resume the original position.	1:30 minutes per side	1:00 minute per side.*

* time is not reduced to less than one minute

HEADSTART FOR HAPPINESS

INHALE

EXHALE

Exercise 2:
Right Facing Arm Raises

Posture/Mudra	Breath	Full Time	1/3 Time
Sit in Easy Pose. Extend the left arm straight out palm facing to the right. Extend the right arm out and cross the right hand under the left. Both palms are facing right, wrap the fingers of the right hand over the left hand so that both palms face right and the fingers lock.	Inhale, raise the arms to 60 degrees and exhale the arms down to parallel to the ground.	2:00-3:00 minutes	1:00 minute*

* time is not reduced to less than one minute

INHALE

EXHALE

Exercise 3:
Arm Swings

Posture/Mudra	Breath	Full Time	1/3 Time
Sit in Easy Pose, bring both arms forward, at the level of the face. The palms do not touch.	Inhale the arms open back and down, exhale the arms forward in front at the level of the face. Breath deep and rhythmic.	3:00 minutes	1:00 minute
Total Time		8:00 to 9:00 minutes	4:00 minutes

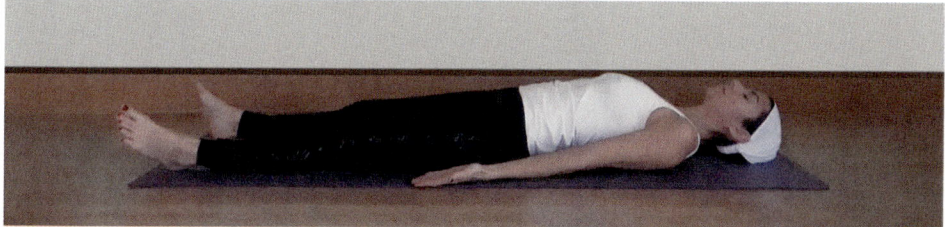

Deep Relaxation:

After you complete a Kundalini Yoga kriya, take a deep relaxation. This is when your body does its deep healing and incorporates some of the energy you have generated through the exercises. The relaxation can last anywhere from two to eleven minutes. To take a deep relaxation, lie on your back with your arms at your sides, palms facing up and relax completely.

Kundalini Yoga Meditation For Type Four Inner Conflict Resolver Reflex

Posture:
Sit in Easy Pose or in a chair with a straight spine and a light neck lock (Jalandhar Bandh).

Mudra:
Place the hands over the chest, with the palms on the torso at the level of the breasts. The fingers point toward each other across the chest.

Eyes:
Close the eyes 9/10 of the way.

Breath:
The key to this meditation is the attention to the breath.
a) Inhale deeply and completely through the nose for 5 seconds.
b) Exhale deeply and completely through the nose for 5 seconds.
c) Hold the breath out for 15 seconds, by suspending the chest motion as you pull in the Navel Point and abdomen.

Mantra:
There is no mantra.

Time:
Start at 3 minutes, work up to 31 minutes.

To End:
Inhale deeply, stretch the hands over the head. Relax the breath and shake the arms and hands for 15-30 seconds. Relax.

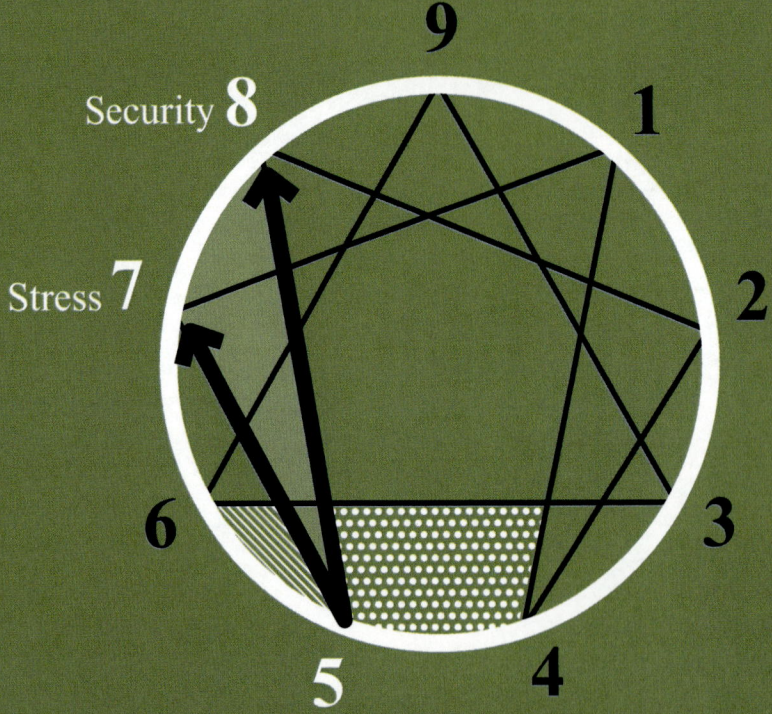

Enneagram Type Five
THE INVESTIGATOR/ THINKER/ OBSERVER

 Overview

Type Five is called the Investigator, the Thinker and the Observer because of their keenly observant, highly curious and inquisitive nature. This person has an ability to focus and concentrate deeply. Type Fives are like the owls of the Enneagram, very observant but usually preferring to stay at the periphery of a situation. Eventually they get bored or lonely and engage more directly by joining the group. But joining the group can be anxiety-provoking for Type Fives as they carefully guard their resources, including energy. A central question in the mind of most Type Fives is "should I engage or should I withdraw?" The tendency is to withdraw. Facts and information serve as guides for what is important to Type Fives.

 Type Five Gifts to the World

Type Fives are the intellectual deep divers of the Enneagram. Their ability to focus, penetrate and go deep into information enables them to create systems, inventions and infrastructures that often benefit the rest of us. Sparks of genius often fuel their inventions, and Type Fives are responsible for some of the most transformative inventions in the world.

Type Fives Typically Report

1) A Desire to Understand Exactly What is Being Asked of Them in a Situation
Type Fives report feeling uncertain and sometimes anxious about being able to meet the needs of others. They like to understand very clearly what is being asked of them in a situation. This desire stems from a concern about resources and a general feeling of scarcity. While there can be exceptions, they generally don't like surprise meetings, unplanned activities, unscheduled assignments or nebulous instructions.

> *"The feeling is like I start each morning with 1/4 of a tank of gas, and I have to figure out how I'm going to make it through the entire day. I'm very aware of who I need to see, how much time it will require, and so forth."*

2) A Strong Need for Time Alone Each Day
Type Fives typically report needing some time alone each day. During this time, they process feelings, they think and recharge, and they reflect on the events of the day. Type Fives typically report they do not have problems establishing personal boundaries with others. They tend to approach the world on their terms, and because of their independent nature and their relative comfort with isolation, they don't easily get swept into doing things they don't want to do.

> *"The idea of not getting time alone each day is almost inconceivable to me. If I don't get it, I'll find it. If I don't find it, I feel like I'll have a nervous breakdown. It is that critical to me."*

3) They Spend a Lot of Time in Their Heads
Type Fives typically report they spend a lot of time in their heads. A highly cerebral type, most Type Fives report they can easily spend hours thinking, studying and reading without interruption. This recharges and nourishes them. They also report that the distance between their head and mouth is very long. They have many thoughts that are never verbalized.

> *"When I was younger, I used to think my body was just a vessel to carry my head around. I really didn't see the point of the body, and I definitely didn't feel connected with mine."*

ENNEAGRAM TYPE FIVE **THE INVESTIGATOR/THINKER/OBSERVER**

 Tools for Compassion If You Have Type Fives in Your Life

1) Understand it is hard for Type Fives to say yes to a request without very careful consideration

Type Fives are keenly aware of resources, including their personal energy, and they often experience concerns about scarcity. Keep this in mind when asking them to do something (a personal favor, a work project). Generally, they will only agree to a request with a lot of thought and analysis. For Type Fives, the instinctive answer for a request or favor is often No. This isn't personal as much as they feel anxious that they don't have what it takes to meet the request. They also report a concern about disappointing the person making the request.

2) Understand it can be difficult for Type Fives to openly discuss emotions

Type Fives often don't know what they are feeling in the moment and need to process the events after the fact to really tune into their emotions. Type Fives are more comfortable in the world of facts and information than in the world of emotion. Because Type Fives have an underlying concern of being overwhelmed, and the emotional world can quickly turn overwhelming, they gravitate away from discussing feelings. It's important to understand this isn't personal, and it doesn't mean they don't care—their minds just move away from the emotional world.

3) Be aware surprises aren't usually a positive thing for most Type Fives

Type Fives like to understand the requirements of each situation. They like to plan, and they don't always like surprises. It can come as a shock to many friends of Type Fives that a surprise visit isn't welcome. Some Type Fives even report hiding when they have an unscheduled visitor at the front door, even if that person is a good friend.

 Next Steps If You are a Type Five

1) Stay engaged in a group, even if it feels a bit uncomfortable

As a Type Five, you are really good at retreating into your head and isolating yourself. Staying in a group environment longer than planned can feel anxiety-provoking for many Type Fives. A good next step is to stay engaged in a group or group activity a little longer than feels comfortable. This helps to enlarge your comfort zone and boundaries.

2) Share something that is more emotion based than fact based

The emotional world tends to be unboundaried, and this feels uncomfortable for most Type Fives. It's like wandering into a situation where the parameters are unestablished and unpredictable. Type Fives also often report they don't know exactly what they are feeling. However, the emotional world is a key part of the human experience. As a Type Five, learning to talk with others about your feelings and emotions is important. A good first step for you might be asking others how they feel about a situation or event. And then try to wait and really listen to what they say. Try to avoid your tendency to apply logic and reasoning to their response.

3) Notice your tendency to stay quiet and reserved. Try to share more

As a Type Five, the distance from your head to your mouth is long, and it is often surprising to others to know how much you actually have to say about a topic. You tend to be very reserved in what you share, and others can experience this as cold, robotic and even stingy. Try to share more of yourself and notice how that changes your interactions with other people.

In the Body (The Energetics of Type Five)

1) Type Fives feel overwhelmed easily and tend to have sensitive nervous systems. Any nervous system work is really helpful for them. Type Fives also tend to feel drained of energy very easily so any physical practice that builds energy is beneficial.

2) Type Fives tend to be very sensitive to their environment and will notice temperature, extra noise, bright lights, etc. more than other types. This stems from concerns about resources and an exaggerated sense that they might become overwhelmed.

3) Type Fives are in their heads so much they often don't consciously connect with their bodies. Any physical practice to get out of their heads and into their bodies can be really helpful.

Take It a Step Further...

The Wings

5w4: The Iconoclast
Type Fives with a Four wing are typically more philosophical, ethereal and poetic than their Six wing counterpart. The Four wing brings an artistic, abstract way of thinking and a creative orientation.

5w6 : The Problem Solver
Type Fives with a Six wing are typically more technical, precise and scientific than their Four wing counterpart. The Six wing brings an analytical, intellectual way of thinking and an orientation towards logic.

Stress and Security Points

Stress Point for Type Five → Type Seven, the Enthusiast/Adventurer/Generalist
When Type Five is under stress, they go to Type Seven, the Enthusiast/Adventurer/Generalist. This makes their behavior more scattered and unfocused, very unlike the typical laser attention for which Type Fives are famous.

Security Point for Type Five → Type Eight, the Leader/Challenger/Protector
When Type Five is feeling relaxed and expansive, they go to Type Eight, the Leader/Challenger/Protector. In this environment, they find their voice, become less reserved and become more direct and forceful in their interactions.

The Subtypes

Self-preservation Type Five: "Castle"
The self-preservation Type Five expresses concerns about resources by having very clearly-drawn boundaries. This is the most guarded, remote and introverted of the Type Fives. This is a person who sometimes describes feeling like he or she "hides." To the outside world, this is someone who may be hermit-like and not overly social. They tend to live very frugally, even if they have plentiful resources. This is the least communicative of the Type Fives. Internally, this is someone who feels a great awareness and concern about scarity and a great drive to live without the trappings of the physical world. They have the title "Castle" because of the way they isolate themselves.

Social Type Five: "Totem"
The social Type Five expresses concerns about resources and boundaries by minimizing the need for emotional connection and in some cases interpersonal relationships in exchange for a pursuit of knowledge. At the core, this is a person who relates less to people than they do to values represented by certain people. To the outside world, this type is more social and engaging than the other Type Fives. This person can become very idealistic or spiritual. Internally, this is a type who is searching for the meaning of life and ultimate ideals. They can feel disinterested in ordinary, everyday life. They have the title "Totem" because of the way they orient around symbols and representations more than actual people and tangible reality.

Intimate Type Five: "Confidence (Confidant)"

The intimate Type Five expresses concerns about resources and scarcity through the search for an ideal partner. This subtype is a more emotional, romantic and sensitive Type Five. Trust is a key issue for this subtype, and the focus for this person can be on finding an ideal partner. To the outside world, this person still appears very boundaried, reserved, observant and emotionally stoic. However, internally this is someone who has a very intense, vivid and romantic emotional life. They feel and suffer a lot, almost resembling the experience of Type Four. They have the title "Confidence" to mean someone who can be confided in. They are given this title because of their search for one ideal partner to bond with completely.

The Kundalini Yoga Kriya and Meditation for Type Five

"All knowledge is false if the soul is not experienced in the body."
~Yogi Bhajan

Kriya: To Balance and Recharge the Nervous and Immune System
Meditation: Wahe Guru Meditation

Type Fives tend to have sensitive nervous systems and can feel overwhelmed easily. They tend to be highly aware of their physical environment and can feel very sensitive to the conditions they are in. A growth opportunity for Type Fives can be to realize they are not as fragile as they imagine they are. "Hiding" from others is a classic Type Five theme, and a growth opportunity for Type Five is to share themselves more.

This Kundalini Yoga kriya builds the nervous and immune system so they feel less overwhelmed and more at ease.

This meditation, with its use of mantra, helps to activate the Fifth Chakra, the Throat Chakra. When this chakra is activated and balanced, it becomes easier for someone to speak their truth, hear their own voice and make their opinions heard.

ENNEAGRAM TYPE FIVE **THE INVESTIGATOR/THINKER/OBSERVER**

Kundalini Yoga Kriya for Type Five
Kriya to Balance and Recharge the Nervous and Immune System
(with One Warm Up Exercise)

Tune In:
Sit in Easy Pose with your legs crossed, bring your hands together in Prayer Pose at your heart center. Tune in and center yourself by chanting "Ong Namo, Guru Dev Namo" three times (see Tuning In on page 32).

Warm Up Exercise:
Ego Eradicator

Posture/Mudra	Breath	Full Time	1/3 Time
Sit in Easy Pose, fingers are pressed into the mounds of the hands, arms at are 60 degrees.	Breath of Fire	3:00 minutes	1:00 minute

HEADSTART FOR HAPPINESS

Exercise 1:
Rapid Left Arm Motion

Posture/Mudra	Breath	Full Time	1/3 Time
Sit in Easy Pose, bring both arms parallel to the ground at 30 degrees forward from the sides in a line with the thighs.	Breathe in rapidly in rhythm with the left arm movement.	11:00 minutes	3:40 minutes
a. Right hand with palm facing forward, keep index and middle finger straight and stiff, bending the fourth and pinkie fingers into the palm, held down by the thumb. The right arm and extended right fingers remain rigid and stiff and do not move throughout the exercise.	Breath will become like a strong Breath of Fire. The eyes are focused on the Third Eye (root of the nose).		
b. Left arm is out with the elbow straight and the palm facing the floor. Fingers are extended. Move the left arm rapidly up and down (about 9 inches/23 centimers total).	To End: Inhale, tense every part of the body, hold the inhale and hold 30 seconds, exhale. Inhale and hold 20 seconds, rapidly exhale. Inhale and hold 5 seconds, exhale and relax.	1:05 minutes	1:05 minutes

Exercise 2:
Hands Pressed at Heart Center

Posture/Mudra	Breath	Full Time	1/3 Time
Sit in Easy Pose. Lock palm over palm with the right palm facing the body, fingers overlapping the back of the opposite hand at level of the Heart Center. Eyes are closed and focused at the Third Eye Point.	Inhale and press hands together so hard that the hands, arms, and rib cage begin to shake. Hold 15 seconds and exhale. Repeat two more times (three times in total). To End: Inhale, hold the breath 10 seconds without pressing the hands, exhale, and relax.	1:00 minute	1:00 minute*
Total Time		16:05 minutes	6:45 minutes

* times are not reduced to less than one minute

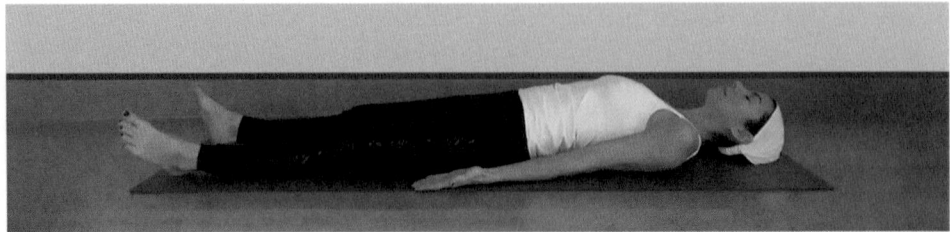

Deep Relaxation:
After you complete the Kundalini Yoga kriya, take a deep relaxation. This is when your body does its deep healing and incorporates some of the energy you have generated through the exercises. The relaxation can last anywhere from two to eleven minutes. To take a deep relaxation, lie on your back with your arms at your sides, palms facing up and relax completely.

ENNEAGRAM TYPE FIVE THE INVESTIGATOR/THINKER/OBSERVER

WAHE

GURU

Kundalini Yoga Meditation for Type Five
Wahe Guru Meditation

Posture:
Sit in Easy Pose with a straight spine and a light neck lock (Jalandhar Bandh).

Mudra:
The hands are in Gyan Mudra (tip of the index finger and tip of the thumb touching). Hands are on the knees, palms facing up.

Eyes:
Eyes are closed.

Breath:
The breath self regulates as you say the mantra.

Mantra:
The mantra is Wahe Guru (pronounced Wha-hay Guroo). A direct translation of the mantra is difficult. Wahe is an expression of ecstasy and Guru is one who brings you from dark to light.

Movement:
Turn your head to the left, bringing your chin over your shoulder as you chant Wahe, then turn your head to the right as you bring your head over your shoulders as you chant Guru. Mentally focus on the union of the lower and higher triangles formed by the tip of the nose and the eyes, and the eyes and the Third Eye Point.

Time:
Start at 3 minutes, work up to 31 minutes.

To End:
Inhale deeply into the center and relax completely.

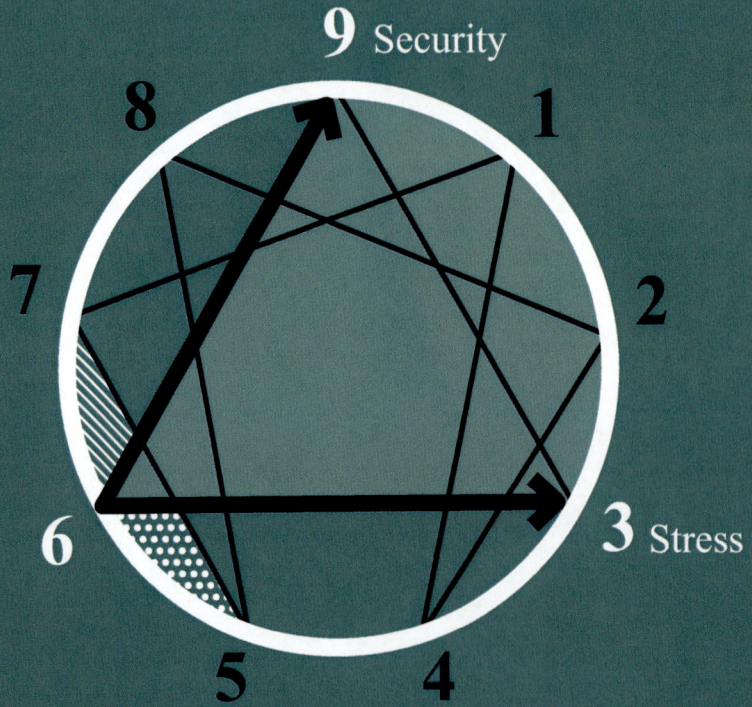

Enneagram Type Six
THE SKEPTIC/ DOUBTER/ LOYALIST

 **Overview**

Type Six is called the Skeptic, the Doubter and the Loyalist because their attention goes to what could go wrong in a situation and because of their intense loyalty and sense of duty. They often struggle with indecision, or they make a decision but as soon as they do, they begin to second guess themselves. They can even second guess their second-guessing. Type Sixes don't put their trust in others easily but once they do, they trust with an almost "go down with the ship" level of loyalty. Type Sixes feel a strong sense of duty and don't shirk responsibility, even when circumstances become challenging.

 Type Six Gifts to the World

Type Sixes are the emergency preparedness kits of the Enneagram. Gifted in foreseeing dangers and problems and proactively planning to address these concerns, Type Sixes keep the rest of us safe. When an actual emergency does arise, Type Sixes are usually grace under pressure, almost as if to say "I've been waiting for this moment my whole life." Type Sixes are deeply loyal and have an unwavering sense of duty. They take their responsibilities seriously and step up, sometimes to their own detriment, to keep commitments and ensure others are cared for.

Type Sixes Typically Report

1) A Heightened Awareness of Danger
Type Sixes are on the lookout for danger and threats to their security. As such, they usually find it. Keenly aware of their physical environment, they spot potential hazards with ease. Characterized as the African gazelles of the Enneagram, this type is on high alert for trouble at all times. This awareness can also be less about the physical environment and more on a psychological or emotional level. Type Sixes are sensitive to perceived threats to their security.

> *"For example, I'm sitting here now in front of you all, and I notice the room is a little warm. I see the person at the back asking the doorman to close the door. And I am thinking if the door is closed, the room will heat up some more. And maybe I'll have problems breathing. In fact, maybe I'll pass out in front of you all, and I won't be able to finish this panel discussion… this goes through my mind."*

2) A Strong Sense of Duty
Type Sixes typically report feeling a strong sense of duty. Like a lieutenant loyal to the general, Type Sixes take their sense of responsibility to family, friends and work very seriously. They can be counted on in difficult situations and often step up when others step back.

> *"My immediate internal response to a need of my family or friends, or even strangers sometimes, is "act now!" It's the same response and sense of urgency as when there is an actual emergency--"go help the situation now!" Often the feelings are so strong that I feel like I'm the ONLY person that can save the day, as though I'm the hero who needs to swoop in and do something."*

> *"This was the case just recently with my father. I made three trips from Greece to Canada to try to resolve a situation he was having. I was determined to go and make the difference because I felt this huge responsibility and duty to step in. This was regardless of the fact there is a long family history involved, and I have two other siblings who are just as responsible for their parent as I am. I felt I was the one who had to change things."*

3) Feeling Anxiety Intensely and Frequently

Most Type Sixes feel anxiety as part of their daily experience. They doubt their choices and decisions, and they even doubt their doubt. Many report procrastinating to make a final decision feeling that when they do, that's when all hell will break loose. Their questioning can be internal or external, but it is frequent. For most Type Sixes, the dangerous scenario they imagine is very real, not a theoretical or mental exercise. They experience the worst case as though the scenes were unfolding before their eyes. Because it feels so real to them, their body and breath is sometimes contracted from feeling stress as though the scenario was actually happening.

> *"If I press send for that final email, that's when the trouble will start. My mind goes to all the things that could go wrong. Sometimes I find myself going in circles. I feel ready to decide, but then I start to doubt my decision. And then I start to doubt my doubt. It is exhausting...."*

> *"I step onto the street and see a bus coming. And like a movie, I see the bus speed up, swerve into me, and how I go flying. It isn't just a general awareness of the bus. It is a vivid, frame-by-frame scenario of me getting hurt. That's what it is like in my mind."*

Tools for Compassion If You Have Type Sixes in Your Life

1) Don't tell them they are overreacting or not to worry
Because Type Sixes are experiencing their imagined worst case scenario as though it is actually happening, telling them not to worry can actually make their anxiety worse. Instead, it is more helpful to calmly go through the worst-case scenario with them step-by-step. This allows them to process the anxiety and to relax.

2) Give them assurance that the relationship is OK
Type Sixes often worry they have jeopardized their relationship with you somehow. Giving them reassurance that the relationship is OK goes a long way in making them feel more secure. This applies even to long-term, highly-stable relationships.

3) Work through issues with them
Type Sixes are loyal and want you to be too. It helps them a lot if you stay by them and work through issues together. Leaving, or threatening to leave, triggers more anxiety and anxious, worst-case scenario thinking.

Next Steps If You are a Type Six

1) Notice your tendency to project into situations
As a Type Six, it is sometimes hard for you to tell where reality ends and where your imagination begins. Your mind has a tendency to magnify and sometimes misinterpret situations. When you begin expanding on the information at hand, notice if you have any actual evidence or if you are following a tendency of anxious thinking.

2) Try to balance the worst-case scenario with more moderate outcomes
As a Type Six, it is easy for your mind to imagine bad outcomes but much harder for your mind to imagine good outcomes. Try to apply some practical logic to the worst-case scenario. Has it actually happened before? How realistic is the worst-case scenario?

3) Try to expand your sphere of experiences and acquaintances
It can be really easy to stay in safe, familiar routines but enlarging your circles can help build confidence. For example, try a new restaurant, travel a different route, make an effort to meet new people. Planned new experiences build confidence and will help make unplanned new experiences feel less threatening.

In the Body (The Energetics of Type Six)

1) Anxiety, worry and doubt are often central issues for Type Sixes. Physically, this can manifest as a contracted stomach or chest. This can also escalate into panic attacks.

2) Hypervigilance and the tension related to being on high alert is a Type Six theme. Type Sixes often carry stress and tension in their shoulders.

3) Shallow breathing can be an issue in Type Sixes. Practice long, deep-belly breathing to help calm and quiet the mind.

Take it a Step Further...

The Wings

6w5: The Defender
Type Sixes with a Five wing are typically more intellectual, introverted and less trusting than their Seven wing counterpart. The Five wing brings desire for self-reliance and a tendency to withdraw.

6w7: The Buddy

Type Sixes with a Seven wing are typically more social, gregarious and seek the support and acceptance of others more than their Five wing counterpart. The Seven wing brings a playfulness, curiosity and cheerful, forward-looking drive.

Stress and Security Points

Stress Point for Type Six → Type Three, the Motivator/Achiever

When Type Six is under stress, they go to Type Three, the Motivator/Achiever. This makes their behavior more competitive and potentially workaholic. Their fear of rejection and loss of security grows, and they may make a more forced attempt to work harder and fit into their surroundings. Their doubt and questioning increases, and they look outside themselves for reassurance and protection.

Security Point for Type Six → Type Nine, the Peacemaker/Mediator

When Type Six is feeling secure, they go to Type Nine, the Peacemaker/Mediator. This makes their behavior more grounded, steady and balanced. They feel an inner stability and don't feel the drive to look outside themselves for support and reassurance. They begin to feel more inclusive of others, even those with differing viewpoints.

The Subtypes

Self-preservation Type Six: "Warmth"

The self-preservation Type Six expresss the drive for security through forming friendships and warm relationships. This is a person who strives to have no enemies and who wants to feel the warmth of a supportive environment. They seek a protective force, someone whom they can rely on for safety, stability and decision-making. To the outside world, this person looks very friendly, warm and pleasant. They are typically in an environment where someone else is making the decisions for them or acting as their protector. Internally, this person feels a great deal of doubt, insecurity and fear. The dependence on an outside "protector" can present almost like separation anxiety, and it can be very hard for this person to connect with his or her own inner guidance. They have the title "Warmth" because of their cultivation of warm relationships.

Social Type Six: "Duty"

The social Type Six expresses the drive for security by aligning with systems and guidelines of conduct. This is a person who finds safety in authority figures and systems (political, religious, family) and often has an underlying fear of disappointing the authority figure. This type often has a philosophical or intellectual way of thinking. They rely less on intuition and feelings and more on their mind. To the outside world, this is someone who is highly reliable, precise in their action and committed to doing the "right" thing. Unlike the self-preservation Type Six who can look very insecure, the social Type Six can look almost too sure. Internally, this person is feeling a great deal of anxiety and insecurity. They feel most secure when things are in clear categories and can have a very hard time with ambiguity. They have the title "Duty" because of their sense of obligation and commitment and their feelings of duty and responsibility.

Intimate Type Six: "Strength/Beauty"
The intimate Type Six expresses the drive for security through cultivating an inner sense of strength. This Type Six wants to come at their fear from a position of power. They go against their fear by rushing at it. They are constantly on the lookout for danger, feeling like it is a dangerous world out there, and anyone could become a threat at any time. To the outside world, this person can look strong, powerful and intimidating. In women, this person looks polished and composed. However, this person is usually also inconsistent and can seem to change their mind and direction frequently. They can be strong, yet weak, decisive, yet indecisive, secure, yet insecure. They have the title "Strength/Beauty" because of their focus on using their power to diffuse their anxiety.

The Kundalini Yoga Kriya and Meditation for Type Six

"The moment you touch your soul, you become fearless."
~Yogi Bhajan

Kriya: For Emotional and Mental Balance
Meditation: For Caliber for Constant Self-Authority

Type Sixes have an overly-developed negative mind and can easily spot danger and threats to security. Cultivating balance, both in thoughts and emotions can be extremely beneficial for this type. Type Sixes tend to be fear-based and look to the outside world for guidance and reassurance. A growth opportunity for Type Six is to cultivate an inner authority and to learn to tune into his or her own higher wisdom.

This Kundalini Yoga kriya brings the person deeply into his or her body and helps to provide balance. Fear is often energetically stored in the hips, and the hip rotations in this kriya can help to release stored fear.

This meditation is designed to increase your capacity for caliber allowing you to tune into, hold and execute self-authority. It increases your abilty to access your own inner guidance.

ENNEAGRAM TYPE SIX THE SKEPTIC/DOUBTER/LOYALIST

Kundalini Yoga Kriya for Type Six
Kriya for Emotional and Mental Balance

Tune In:
Sit in Easy Pose with your legs crossed, bring your hands together in Prayer Pose at your heart center. Tune in and center yourself by chanting "Ong Namo, Guru Dev Namo" three times (see Tuning In on page 32).

Exercise 1:
Miracle Bend

Posture/Mudra	Breath	Full Time	1/3 Time
In a standing position with knees and heels together, feet are flat on the ground, with the big toes pointing out to the sides for balance.	Keep the breath long, deep and gentle.	2:00 minutes	1:00 minute*
Arms are raised straight overhead, close to the ears with the palms facing forward (thumbs can be locked together).			
Keeping the legs straight, bend back from the base of the spine 20 degrees. The head, spine and arms form an unbroken curve with the arms remaining in a line with the ears. Hold the posture.			
This exercise bends the negativity of a human being and helps bring an emotional or angry person to calmness.			

* time is not reduced to less than 1:00 minute

Exercise 2:
Forward Bend

Posture/Mudra	Breath	Full Time	1/3 Time*
From the position in Exercise 1, very slowly bend forward, keeping the arms straight and close to the ears. Stay down.	Stay down in the position and inhale. Hold the breath as long as possible and pump the navel point. Exhale and pump the navel point. Hold out the exhale. Continue this breath pattern.	2:00 minutes	1:00 minute*

* time is not reduced to less than 1:00 minute

Exercise 3:
Hip Rotation

Posture/Mudra	Breath	Full Time	1/3 Time
In a standing position, spread the legs as wide apart as possible without losing balance.	Let the breath find its own rhythm.	2:00 minutes	1:00 minute*
Bend the elbows and have the forearms more or less parallel to the ground.			
Begin rotating the hips at a moderate pace in as complete and large circles as possible. The direction can be either to the left or the right.			
This exercise will raise the spirit, correct any victim mentality and give the will to fight and not give in.			

* time is not reduced to less than 1:00 minute

Exercise 4:
Arm Rotations

Posture/Mudra	Breath	Full Time	1/3 Time
Maintain the same leg position as in Exercise 3 but straighten the arms.	Let the breath find its own rhythm.	1:30 minutes	1:00 minute*
Begin a backward and alternate rotation of the arms, never bring the arms more than 30 degrees in towards the body. The rhythm is one rotation of the arm per second.			
While rotating the arms, bend forward from the waist half way, straighten up again, and then bend backward from the waist.			
The rhythm is 15 seconds per complete cycle.			

* time is not reduced to less than 1:00 minute

Exercise 5:
Deep Relaxation

Posture/Mudra	Breath	Full Time	1/3 Time
Deep relaxation	Let the breath find its own rhythm.	10:00 minutes	3:20 minutes
Total time		17:30 minutes	7:20 minutes

* Because this Kundalini Yoga kriya includes a deep relaxation in the set, a second relaxation can be added or omitted. Total deep relaxation time typically doesn't exceed eleven minutes.

ENNEAGRAM TYPE SIX THE SKEPTIC/DOUBTER/LOYALIST

Kundalini Yoga Meditation for Type Six
Meditation for Caliber for Constant Self-Authority

Posture:
Sit in Easy Pose with a straight spine and a light neck lock (Jalandhar Bandh). Keep torso straight at all times (don't lean forward or back).

Mudra:
Bring the hands in front of the body at the level of the Heart Center. Close the fingers over the thumbs into fists with the thumb tips at the base of the little fingers, if possible. Press the fists together at the first knuckles from the tips of the fingers so that the base of the palms are together and the backs of the palms face way from the center.

Eyes:
Eyes are fixed on the tip of the nose.

Breath:
Begin the following steady breathing pattern:
   1) inhale deeply through the nose
   2) exhale deeply through the mouth with pursed lips
   3) inhale smoothly through the mouth
   4) exhale through the nose

Mantra:
There is no mantra.

Time:
Start at 3 minutes, work up to 22 minutes.

To End:
Inhale and hold the breath as you stretch both hands up over the head. Exhale and continue to stretch for 2 more breaths. Relax.

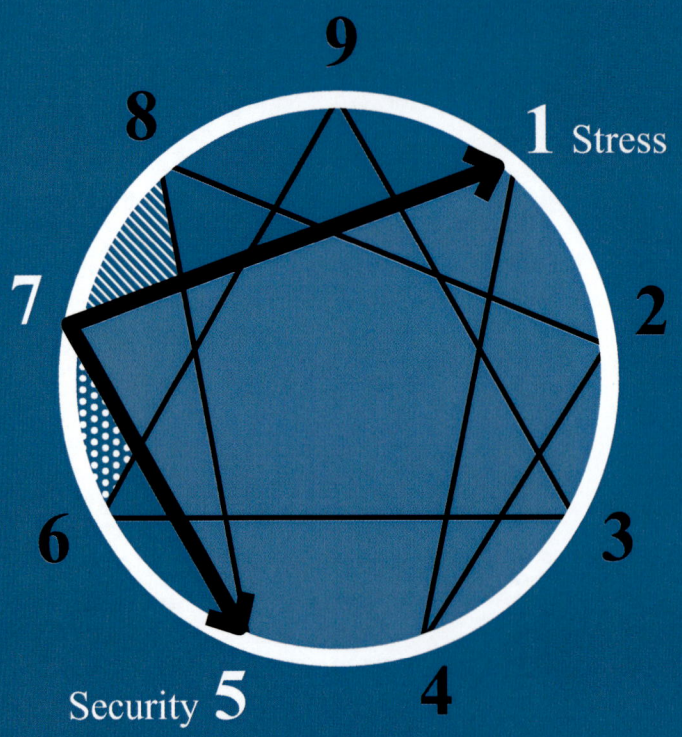

Enneagram Type Seven
THE ENTHUSIAST/ ADVENTURER/ GENERALIST

 **Overview**

Type Seven is called the Enthusiast, the Adventurer and the Generalist because of their enthusiasm for almost everything (especially new things), their adventure-seeking focus and their wide range of interests. Upbeat, high energy and curious, this is an action-oriented type who places a lot of focus on enjoyment, being happy and future planning. This is a person whose attention goes to what is fun, pleasing and enjoyable. Their attention moves away from anything that might lead to negative emotions. Type Sevens typically don't like rules and limitations. Personal freedom is a big priority.

 Type Seven Gifts to the World

Type Sevens bring the gifts of joy, positivity, gratitude and playfulness. Naturally oriented to see the positive, Type Sevens are capable of profound awe, delight and wonder of the world. Their upbeat energy can brighten even the darkest environment, and they are naturally uplifting to others.

Type Sevens Typically Report

1) Having Great Difficulty Narrowing Down Their Choices—They Want It All

Type Sevens are on an endless quest to find what will make them happy. Since they aren't quite sure what that is, they want to try everything. The idea of missing out on something can be anxiety-provoking, as their mind considers "what if that was the thing that I was really going to love?"

> *"I once stayed in a hotel that had a really big buffet. I literally ate until I was sick, because I had to try everything. I still remember feeling very full, but eating more and more because there were dishes I hadn't tried yet…"*

2) Disliking Limitations and Rules

Type Sevens want freedom so they have space to pursue whatever might make them happy. They gravitate away from rules, limitations and anything that might pen them in. Restrictions and limiting their options triggers an anxiety response in most Type Sevens.

> *"For most of my career, I've worked for myself or in environments where my bosses gave me a lot of freedom and autonomy. Having a microman-ager and being in really strict work environments is awful for me. I feel like I'm running out of oxygen…I've had it happen twice in my career, and both times I quit the job within six months. It just wasn't worth it."*

3) An Avoidance of Negative Emotions

"Why feel bad?" is the mantra of Type Seven, and negative emotions can feel very threatening to them. This type generally avoids dwelling in the negative. If something unavoidably negative happens, they might acknowledge it briefly, but they quickly reframe the negative event into something positive. Underneath it all is a deep instinct that "if I start feeling bad, I may never stop…" Type Sevens can experience negative emotions like the threat of falling into a bottomless pit. As such, they work very hard not to feel bad.

> *"My mind can reframe anything, and it does automatically, without me even trying. Yes, I was fired from my job and that's bad, but I didn't like that work anyway and look at all the other options I have now."*

Tools for Compassion If You Have Type Sevens in Your Life

1) Recognize that staying with negative emotions is extremely difficult for them

Type Sevens have great difficulty staying with negative emotions. They automatically reframe the negative to positive, which can be frustrating to the other people in their lives. It is important to recognize they aren't trying to be insensitive or to ignore the difficulty. They become anxious if they stay in negative emotions too long.

2) Don't think that all their wild plans will actually happen. It is mainly a pleasant mental exercise for them

Type Sevens get great pleasure in planning future enjoyable activities. They aren't famous for their follow through and don't really expect all the plans to materialize anyway. It is the planning, imagining and discussing that they really enjoy. Understanding that many of the plans will never materialize is important, particularly for more serious types who might think they will need to be involved in the execution of some of the plans.

3) Personal freedom gives them a sense of security

Type Sevens feel secure when they have a lot of personal freedom. Strict rules, rigid limitations and anything that eliminates options can be anxiety-provoking and often cause Type Sevens to act out. They function better in environments where they are given a lot of free rein and flexibility. They can be extremely committed (to relationships, jobs, projects) but typically this commitment must also allow a Type Seven to continue to feel free and independent. The sense of freedom lowers the underlying anxiety in Type Sevens and counterintuitively, this sense of freedom makes it easier for them to commit.

In the Body (The Energetics of Type Seven)

1) Type Sevens have monkey mind and often report it is difficult to concentrate or focus on something for an extended period of time. Their minds move quickly, and they can feel scattered.

2) Type Sevens generally have high energy, and energy containment can be an issue. They experience a rush of excitement at the thought of a new idea, adventure or experience and can literally get "carried away" by the energy.

3) Though less obvious, Type Sevens are also head/mental types and go into their minds to solve problems. While they are often very physically active, they can be very discon-

nected from their bodies. Any breathwork or slower physical activity that connects them to their body is really helpful.

Next Steps If You are a Type Seven

1) Slow down!
As a Type Seven, you likely have boundless energy and tend to have a very full schedule. Try to spend a quiet night or two at home without talking with friends or having distractions in the background. Quiet environments can let emotions arise.

2) Try not to start new projects or pursue new ideas until you finish the old ones
As a Type Seven, you love new projects and ideas. However, you also have a tendency to get distracted when the project becomes difficult or challenging. Your attention naturally goes to the next thing to try. Staying focused and working through negativity is important so try to finish existing projects before starting new ones.

3) Learn discernment
As a Type Seven, you can become enthusiastic about most new things. However, all things are not equally beneficial. Try to think of what will really bring you fulfillment and not just something that is new. Seeking fulfillment over enjoyment will help you stay focused.

Take It a Step Further...

The Wings

7w6 : The Entertainer
Type Sevens with a Six wing are more relationship-oriented, insecure and openly vulnerable than their Eight wing counterparts. The Six wing brings a sense of responsibility, a loyalty, an often visible sense of anxiety and a sense of humor.

7w8 : The Realist
Type Sevens with an Eight wing are more adventurous, bold, direct and protective of others than their Six wing counterparts. The Eight wing brings big energy, a brashness and lust for life.

Stress and Security Points

Stress Point for Type Seven → Type One, the Perfectionist/Reformer

When Type Seven is under stress, they go to Type One, the Perfectionist/Reformer. This makes their behavior much more rigid and perfectionist. They can come across as strict and stern when under pressure.

Security Point for Type Seven → Type Five, the Investigator/Thinker/Observer

When Type Seven is feeling more secure, relaxed, and expansive, they go to Type Five, the Investigator/Thinker/Observer. This makes their behavior more focused, reserved and less manic. They enjoy a bit of solitude and don't look to the outside environment to supply an endless amount of stimulation.

The Subtypes

Self-preservation Seven: "Keeper of the Castle"

The self-preservation Type Seven expresses gluttony and a drive for new experiences by finding opportunities to leverage and expand their network. This is a person who typically has a large circle of friends and contacts and acts as a connector or influencer to leverage this circle. Earthy, practical, driven and sometimes self-interested, this Type Seven is often professionally accomplished and successful. This type has the title "Keeper of the Castle" because of their cultivation of a gang or self-created family, within which they occupy a key role.

Social Type Seven: "Sacrifice"

The social Type Seven counters guttony and a drive for new experiences by consciously trying to control their urge for more. This is a person who often puts the needs of others ahead of their own needs and often focuses their energy into a social cause or support of the family. Generous, idealistic, active and often naive, this type has the title "Sacrifice" because of their tendency to subvert their own desires for the greater good.

Intimate Type Seven: "Fascination"

The intimate Type Seven expresses gluttony and a drive for new experiences by embellishing reality to see it as much more positive and vivid than it actually is. Their mind overemphasizes the positive data leaving this Type Seven "trapped in sunshine." This is a person who genuinely experiences the world as an amazing place filled with endless potential for positive experiences and encounters. Less grounded than the other Type Sevens, this type is more interested in things of a higher world, the metaphysical, intellectual or philosophical. They have the title "Fascination" because they experience the world with intense fascination and enthusiasm.

The Kundalini Yoga Kriya and Meditation for Type Seven

"Life is a chance to commit, and commitment means to go through it, to complete it. It is an experience."
~Yogi Bhajan

Kriya: To Purify The Self
Meditation: Caliber of Life

Type Sevens have "monkey mind" meaning their minds tend to race, and they are easily distracted. This type tends to have a lot of energy, and energy containment can be a big issue. The growth path for Type Seven is to learn to focus, to stay with difficult things and to learn discernment, the ability to tell the difference between what is good for them and what is just new for them.

This Kundalini Yoga kriya helps to address the Type Seven issue of energy management by bringing them fully into their body. The first and fourth exercises in this kriya are physically challenging and require mental focus. The second, third, and fifth exercises require focused breathwork, which leads to better focus and control of the mind. And all the exercises have a connection to the heart, which is helpful for Type Sevens.

This meditation includes a physical challenge in keeping the arms outstretched, a mental challenge in keeping up with the breath and a visual challenge in that the eyes remain open and fixed on a specific spot. Combined, these elements help Type Seven to grow.

Kundalini Yoga Kriya for Type Seven
Kriya To Purify The Self
(with One Warm Up Exercise)

Tune In:
Sit in Easy Pose with your legs crossed, bring your hands together in Prayer Pose at your heart center. Tune in and center yourself by chanting "Ong Namo, Guru Dev Namo" three times (see Tuning In on page 32).

Warm Up Exercise:
Left Nostril Breathing

Posture/Mudra	Breath	Full Time	1/3 Time
Sit with a straight spine.	Long deep breathing.	3:00 minutes	1:00 minute
Block the right nostril gently with the index finger of the right hand. Inhale and exhale slowly through your left nostril.			

Exercise 1:
Standing Lunge

Posture/Mudra	Breath	Full Time	1/3 Time
Stand up. Extend one leg back as far as you can with the top of the foot on the ground; the opposite knee bends until the thigh is almost parallel with the ground. Most of the pressure will be on the bent leg. Put the palms together at the center of the chest. Focus at the Brow Point	In this position, take 3 deep breaths, holding the inhalation for about 8 seconds each time. Come back to standing and switch to the opposite leg and take 3 deep breaths on this side, holding the inhalation for about 8 seconds each time. Repeat twice more on each side	3 repetitions on each side	2 repetitions on each side*

* repetitions are not reduced below 2 repetitions in this kriya

ENNEAGRAM TYPE SEVEN **THE ENTHUSIAST/ADVENTURER/GENERALIST**

Exercise 2:
Diaphragm Lift

Posture/Mudra	Breath	Full Time	1/3 Time
Sit in Easy Pose. Place the hands on the hips. Lift the diaphragm high. Raise both shoulders as high as possible. Inhale and exhale very deeply while holding this posture.	Inhale and exhale very deeply while holding this posture.	2:00-3:00 minutes	1:00 minute*

* time is not reduced to less than 1:00 minute

Exercise 3:
Bear Grip

Posture/Mudra	Breath	Full Time	1/3 Time
Sit in Easy Pose, and bring the hands into Bear Grip (hook the fingers together at the center of the chest) with the right palm facing down. Forearms and elbows are parallel to the ground.	Inhale deeply. Exhale forcefully and completely and apply mulbandh. Inhale-hold the breath, apply mulbandh and mentally raise the pranic energy from the base of the spine to the crown.	3:00 minutes	1:00 minute

Exercise 4:
Arms Extended

Posture/Mudra	Breath	Full Time	1/3 Time
Sit in Easy Pose, Extend the arms out the sides, parallel to the ground. Press the palms out with the fingers pointing up. Roll the eyes up and focus at the Brow Point.	Inhale deeply-hold the breath while applying a firm mulbandh for 20 seconds. Then exhale and repeat.	2:00-3:00 minutes	1:00 minute*

* time is not reduced to less than 1:00 minute

ENNEAGRAM TYPE SEVEN **THE ENTHUSIAST/ADVENTURER/GENERALIST**

Exercise 5:
Hands in Prayer Pose in Front of Chest

Posture/Mudra	Breath	Full Time	1/3 Time
In Easy Pose, press the palms together-about 2-3 inches (or 5-8 centimeters) in front of the chest-with the fingers pointing up. Pull the spine straight. Press with 30-50 pounds (or 14-23 kilos) of pressure.	Let the breath find its own rhythm.	2:00 minutes	1:00 minute*
Total Time		12:00-14:00 minutes	6:00 minutes

* time is not reduced to less than 1:00 minute

Deep Relaxation:

After you complete the Kundalini Yoga kriya, take a deep relaxation. This is when your body does its deep healing and incorporates some of the energy you have generated through the exercises. The relaxation can last anywhere from two to eleven minutes. To take a deep relaxation, lie on your back with your arms at your sides, palms facing up and relax completely.

Kundalini Yoga Meditation for Type Seven
Caliber of Life Meditation

Posture:
Sit in Easy Pose with a straight spine and a light neck lock (Jalandhar Bandh).

Mudra:
Extend the arms straight out in front, parallel to the ground. Close the right hand into a fist. Wrap the left fingers around the right fist. The base of the palms touch, thumbs are extended up and touch along the sides.

Eyes:
Eyes are focused on the thumbnails and through the "V" (like you are using it to view a target).

Breath:
All breathing is done through the nose.

    1) inhale for 5 seconds

    2) exhale for 5 seconds

    3) suspend (hold) the breath out for 15 seconds

Mantra:
There is no mantra.

Time:
Start at 3 minutes, work up to 11 minutes. Do not exceed 11 minutes.

To End:
Inhale deeply and slowly lower the arms.

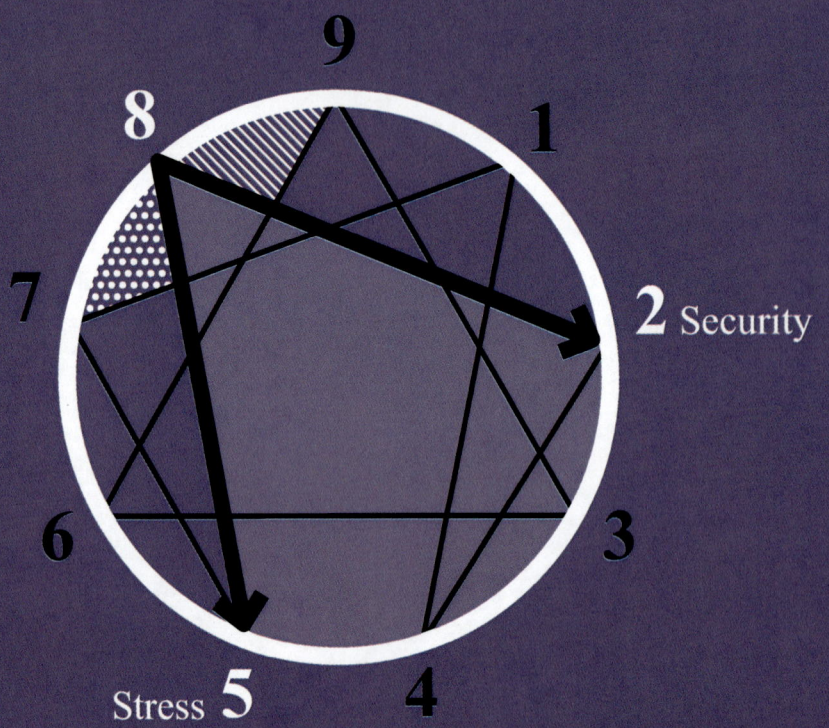

Enneagram Type Eight
THE LEADER/ CHALLENGER/ PROTECTOR

 **Overview**

The Type Eight is called the Leader, the Challenger and the Protector because of their keen awareness of power dynamics: who is in control, who might need protection, who needs to be challenged. Type Eights are usually blunt, direct, "what you see is what you get" people with forceful, big personalities. Sometimes described as a bull in a china shop, Type Eights often get feedback at some point in their life that they are just too much for people or that they overwhelm others. Sharing vulnerable, softer emotions can be challenging for Type Eights who are typically not comfortable expressing anything that feels like weakness.

 Type Eight Gifts to the World

Type Eights bring the world leadership, resourcefulness, an interest in fairness and equality and protection for the underdog. Natural leaders, this type is decisive, strong and resourceful. Extremely tough, they keep going long after other people give up. The soldiers of the Enneagram, Type Eights defend the weak, vulnerable and underprivileged.

Type Eights Typically Report

1) They Access Anger Easily

Type Eights tend to over express anger. They report that anger comes up so fast, it feels almost impossible to stop even though they often regret the consequences. This anger is typically linked to feeling vulnerable, although most Type Eights don't experience it that way.

> *"I have literally seen red I've been so angry. I've been counseled at work that my anger is intimidating my coworkers, so I know I need to control it, but it's hard. It just comes up so fast…"*

2) Sharing Vulnerable Emotions is Difficult

Sharing anything that makes them feel vulnerable is challenging for Type Eights. Their instinct is that the world isn't a safe place and letting your guard down is dangerous. This type typically shuts down and goes into isolation when they are feeling hurt or sad and returns later when they are feeling less vulnerable. Because being vulnerable is so hard for Type Eights, they can sometimes have issues with intimacy.

> *"I remember I was eleven years old and watching E.T. at the movie theatre. There was the really emotional scene where E.T. wanted to contact home. And my entire body was clenched so I wouldn't cry because it was so important not to cry in a theatre with other people around me."*

3) They Think about Revenge

Type Eights think a lot about revenge, even though they may not actually act on it. They spend time mentally planning and imagining how they will right the wrong someone did to them or someone or something they care about. In some more extreme instances, they may act on it, but often the fantasy is enough.

> *"I have imagined blowing up buildings and destroying three generations of a family because one member did something that really pissed me off. And this isn't just imagining I'd do it, I was thinking of what explosives I would need, where I would get them, and so forth. Of course in the end, I didn't and wouldn't act on it. But it took up space in my mind…"*

Tools for Compassion If You Have Type Eights in Your Life

1) Don't Take Their Aggressive Speech Personally
Type Eights are often extremely direct, blunt and sometimes loud and forceful. Their aggressive speech style can overwhelm others without them even realizing it. To the Type Eight, they are just being themselves, participating in the group. To others, they are intimidating.

> *"I started to understand there was a problem because I'd go to parties and immediately gravitate to where the energy was biggest and the conversation was the most lively. But after a few minutes of me arriving, people would start drifting away. And eventually I'd be all alone in the room. This happened repeatedly so I knew it must be something I was doing wrong…"*

2) Understand They Use Confrontation as a Measure of Where They Stand
Type Eights are often confrontational as a way to understand their environment. This is automatic behavior for them, and counterintuitively Type Eights relax more when the other person pushes back. Direct confrontation is much more comfortable for them than passive aggressive or falsely submissive behavior.

> *"If someone doesn't push back, I feel like I am punching a cloud. I have no idea where I stand or what to expect from the person. It's really uncomfortable for me…"*

3) Their Anger Isn't Usually About What It's About
It can be helpful to understand that Type Eights get angry in response to feeling vulnerable. When an angry episode is unpackaged, the root cause is usually that the Type Eight felt vulnerable, defenseless or exposed.

> *"I was talking with my wife, and at some point I realized she walking through a parking lot alone. And as I started to question her about it, I became angrier and angrier until I was actually screaming at her on the phone. Much later, I realized it was because I was afraid something might happen to her. But in the moment, I just felt angry, and she experienced me screaming at her."*

Next Steps If You are a Type Eight

1) Take Some Time Each Day To Self-Nurture
As a Type Eight, you often underestimate your own physical needs. Many Type Eights push their bodies hard and often later in life have health issues because of years of neglect. Try to spend a few minutes each day checking in with yourself about how your body physically feels. Do some basic self-nurturing daily (neck rolls can be a really good start).

2) Use Your Breath to Manage Your Anger Response
It is likely you feel the energy of anger fairly easily. Learning to manage this response is important. A practice of long deep breathing every day can help to create space for choice between the rush of anger and actual action. Long deep breathing automatically lowers tension.

3) Understand that Sharing Vulnerable Emotions Will Cultivate Closer Releationships
Type Eights often report they are lonely. As a naturally aggressive personality, they inadvertently push people away and unconsciously present themselves as strong, self-reliant, and not needing support. This behavior blocks more intimate connection. As a Type Eight try to share some of your more vulnerable feelings (sadness, fear, insecurity). Learning to share vulnerability can go a long way towards cultivating closer relationships.

In the Body (The Energetics of Type Eight)

1) As described above, Type Eights have a tendency to underestimate their own physical needs, particularly as it relates to self-nurturing and often push themselves too hard. Their bodies typically carry a lot of strain and tension, particularly in the neck and shoulders.

2) Type Eights sometimes disregard or dismiss the emotional world. They can have difficulty getting in touch with their softer emotions. They have a lot of "body armor" around the heart chakra. Any heart-opening work is really good for Type Eights.

3) Type Eights often go to anger to protect from feeling more vulnerable emotions. Slowing down the anger response can be very helpful.

Take It a Step Further...

The Wings

8w7: The Maverick
Type Eights with a Seven wing are typically more extroverted and social, with a lighter touch and a larger sense of adventure than their Nine wing counterparts. The Seven wing brings joy, an upbeat energy and enthusiasm.

8w9: The Bear
Type Eights with a Nine wing are typically more calm, home-oriented and introverted with a tighter social circle than their Seven wing counterparts. The Nine wing brings a sense of tolerance, informality and patience.

Stress and Security Points

Stress Point for Type Eight → Type Five, the Investigator/Thinker/Observer
When Type Eight is under stress, they go to Type Five, the Investigator/Thinker/Observer. This makes their behavior more withdrawn, isolated and thoughtful. The normally big energy Type Eight becomes more consolidated with his or her energy and resources and often retreats from the world.

Security Point for Type Eight → Type Two, the Helper/Giver/Lover
When Type Eight is feeling relaxed and expansive, they go to Type Two, the Helper/Giver/Lover. This makes their behavior more magnanimous, helpful and altruistic. In this environment, Type Eights take their energy and leadership skills and focus these resources to help others.

The Subtypes

Self-preservation Type Eight: "Satisfaction"
The self-preservation Type Eight expresses lust and aggression on the most basic level. Strong, powerful, direct and productive, this is a person who likes material comfort, good food and drink and good company. To the outside world, this looks like a no-nonsense personality who dislikes pretense and who pursues what he or she wants without much, if any, hesitation. Internally, there is an instinct that they must act to fulfill their needs. They have the title "Satisfaction" because of their direct drive for personal satisfaction of their desires.

Social Type Eight: "Solidarity"

The social Type Eight expresses lust and aggression on a more muted level than the other two subtypes. The least angry of the Type Eights, this person tends to align with groups and can have a more difficult time with individualized relationships. To the outside world, this is a person who is nurturing, protective, loyal, friendly and highly concerned with injustices that happen to the weak or underprivileged. Internally, this is someone who has a hard time nurturing his or her own needs and moves towards the power of the group to have his or her needs met. They have the title "Solidarity" because of their alignment around groups and their quest for loyalty.

Intimate Type Eight: "Possession"

The intimate Type Eight expresses lust and aggression through open rebellion. The most emotional and least conventional of the Type Eights, this person feels things deeply and tends to be more action-oriented than contemplative. To the outside world, this is a highly magnetic, charismatic person who energetically takes over his or her environment. Internally, this type has a sense that the world starts when they enter the room. They have the title "Possession" because of their tendency to have possessive relationships with lovers, friends, places, objects and situations.

The Kundalini Yoga Kriya and Meditation for Type Eight

"Just wait. Don't react. Therein lies the whole universe. Just don't react."
~Yogi Bhajan

Kriya: To Open the Heart
Meditation: One Minute Breath

Type Eights typically overexpress anger and underexpress (and undervalue) the more vulnerable emotions like sadness, fear, melancholy and anxiety. A growth opportunity for Type Eight is to learn to slow down the anger reaction, connect more fully to their heart and express their more vulnerable emotions.

The Kundalini Yoga kriya To Open the Heart is designed to shed some of the emotional and energetic body armor that surrounds the heart center, allowing the heart to open and a wider range of emotions to be felt. It is a beautiful kriya that includes exercises vigorous enough to keep Type Eights engaged but gentle enough to allow real healing to take place.

One Minute Breath develops the ability to slow the breath on command. A slower breath automatically slows down the reaction time from the emotional rush of the energy of anger. It gives the person an opportunity to act, not react. This breath technique is helpful as an anger management tool and gives you the space of choice in your actions.

ENNEAGRAM TYPE EIGHT THE LEADER/CHALLENGER/PROTECTOR

Kundalini Yoga Kriya for Type Eight
Kriya to Open the Heart
(with One Warm Up Exercise)

Tune In:
Sit in Easy Pose with your legs crossed, bring your hands together in Prayer Pose at your heart center. Tune in and center yourself by chanting "Ong Namo, Guru Dev Namo" three times (see Tuning In on page 32).

Warm Up Exercise:
Neck Rolls

Posture/Mudra	Breath	Full Time	1/3 Time
Slowly rotate the head about the neck.	Let the breath find its own rhythm	3:00 minutes	1:00 minute

Exercise 1:
Prayer Pose with Breath of Fire

Posture/Mudra	Breath	Full Time	1/3 Time
Stand with palms together in Prayer Pose at the center of the chest and do a steady Breath of Fire.	Breath of Fire	3:00 minutes	1:00 minute
To End: Inhale and hold briefly.			

Exercise 2:
Punching Fists

Posture/Mudra	Breath	Full Time	1/3 Time
Stand or sit with an erect spine. Keep the eyes open and look to the horizon. Make fists of both hands. Begin alternately punching with one fist then the other. Together the hands create a piston-like motion with one arm pulling back to balance the other arm punching forward. The hands do not turn or twist.	Exhale with each punch forward and punch rapidly so the breath becomes like a Breath of Fire.	3:00 minutes	1:00 minute
To End: Inhale, draw both elbows back, tighten the fists, apply root lock, and suspend the breath for 5 seconds. Exhale and relax.			

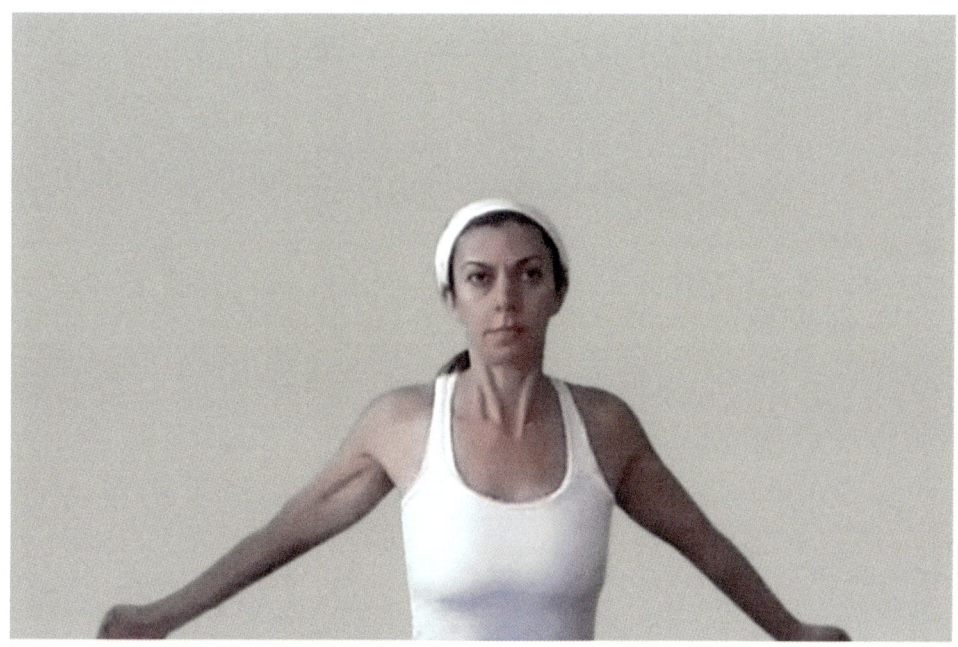

Exercise 3:
Standing Arm Circles

Posture/Mudra	Breath	Full Time	1/3 Time
Stand straight, extend the arms out to the sides, and begin to make big circles with both arms at the same time. Inhale as they come forward and up, and exhale as they go back and down.	Inhale as arms come forward and up, and exhale as arms go back and down.	2:00 minutes	1:00 minute*
To End: Inhale and stretch both arms straight up over the head. Exhale and relax.			

* time is not reduced to less than 1:00 minute

EXERCISE 4A EXERCISE 4B EXERCISE 4C

Exercise 4:
Arm Pumps

Posture/Mudra	Breath	Full Time	1/3 Time
Sit straight.	Create a steady pumping motion with a powerful breath	3:00 minutes	1:00 minute
Interlace the fingers with the thumbtips touching. **a.** Position the hands 4-6 inches (10-15 centimeters) in front of the chest with both palms facing down. Lift the elbows to the same level.			
b. Inhale as you lift the hands up to the level of the throat.			
c. Exhale as you sweep them down to the level of the Navel.			
To End: Inhale, bring the hands to the level of the heart, and suspend the breath for 10 seconds. Exhale and relax.			

ENNEAGRAM TYPE EIGHT THE LEADER/CHALLENGER/PROTECTOR

Exercise 5:
Arms to Side, Mentally Vibrate SA TA NA MA with Finger Motion

Posture/Mudra	Breath	Full Time	1/3 Time
Stand or sit with a straight spine.	Slowly inhale and exhale. Your breath should be equal on the inhale and the exhale	3:00-5:00 minutes	1:00-1:40 minutes
Place the hands beside the shoulders with elbows by your sides and palms facing forward. Close your eyelids halfway and fix your gaze downward.			
Mentally repeat the following primal sound scale on both the inhale and exhale: Saa Taa Naa Maa			
Press the thumb tips to the finger tips sequentially from the first finger tip to the little finger tip with Saa Taa Naa Maa, while you vibrate the mental sounds, as you would with Kirtan Kriya.			

Exercise 6:
Left Nostril Breathing

Posture/Mudra	Breath	Full Time	1/3 Time
Sit with a straight spine.	Match the duration of the inhale and exhale, with each one lasting about 10 seconds.	3:00 minutes slow breathing, then 2:00 minutes with the natural flow of the breath.	1:00 minute slow breathing then 1:00 minute with the natural flow of the breath.*
Block the right nostril gently with the index finger of the right hand.			
Inhale slowly through your left nostril, exhale slowly through rounded lips.			
Total Time		21:00-23:00 minutes	8:00-8:40 minutes

* time is not reduced to less than 1:00 minute

Deep Relaxation:
After you complete the Kundalini Yoga kriya, take a deep relaxation. This is when your body does its deep healing and incorporates some of the energy you have generated through the exercises. The relaxation can last anywhere from two to eleven minutes. To take a deep relaxation, lie on your back with your arms at your sides, palms facing up and relax completely.

ENNEAGRAM TYPE EIGHT THE LEADER/CHALLENGER/PROTECTOR

"If you can breathe one breath a minute, you can overcome everything and anything you have to face in life."

~Yogi Bhajan

Kundalini Yoga Meditation for Type Eight
One Minute Breath

Posture:
Sit in Easy Pose with a straight spine and a light neck lock (Jalandhar Bandh).

Mudra:
Hands are relaxed either in your lap or in Gyan Mudra with the hands on the knees palms facing up.

Eyes:
Unspecified. Eyes can be open or closed.

Breath:
All breathing is done through the nose. Begin with 30-60 seconds of long deep breathing as a warm up for One Minute Breath.

  a) Inhale for 20 seconds. Breathe slowly and deeply, drawing air first into your lower, then middle, and finally upper lungs so that the entire lung is participating.

  b) Suspend/hold the breath for 20 seconds.

  c) Exhale for 20 seconds.

Mantra:
There is no mantra.

Time:
Start at 3 minutes, work up to 31 minutes.

To End:
Inhale deeply and relax.

Teaching Comments:
Take your time with this pranayama, building your way slowly to the full 20 second inhale/hold/exhale cycle. If you cannot do 20 seconds, then do 10 or even 5 seconds. Just be sure to keep the breath even, and inhale/hold/exhale for the same amount of time. Example: Inhale 5 seconds, hold 5 seconds, exhale 5 seconds.

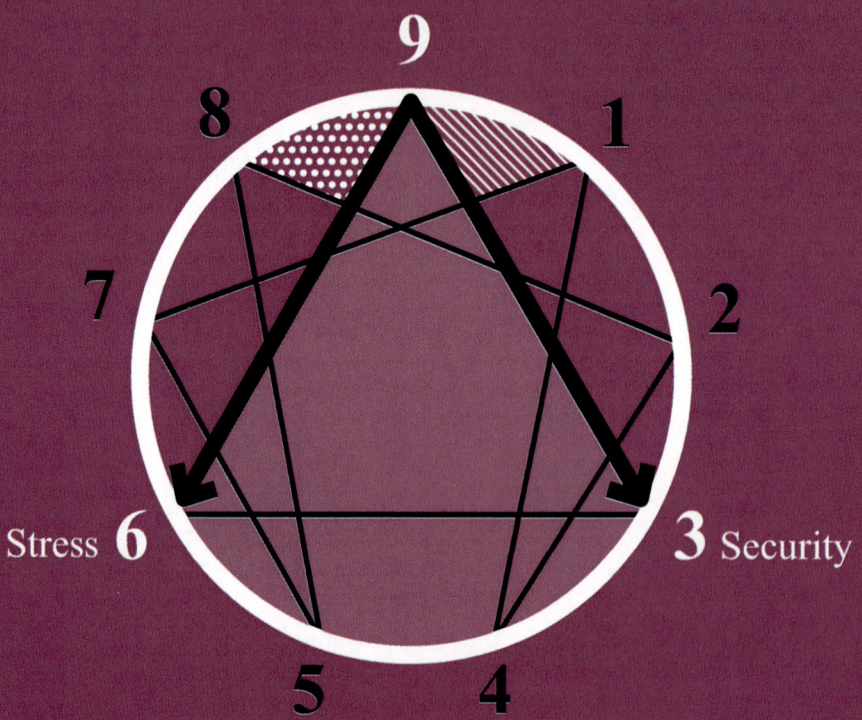

Enneagram Type Nine
THE PEACEMAKER/ MEDIATOR

 **Overview**

Type Nine is called the Peacemaker or the Meditator because of their focus on harmony and their mellow, go with the flow attitude. Type Nines are naturally able to understand multiple perspectives and are exceptional listeners. They offer a non-judgmental environment that allows others to be heard and often de-escalate highly-charged situations. Type Nines are so good at understanding the position of others that they sometimes "forget" themselves and lose their own perspectives and agendas. Many Type Nines reach a point in their life where they look up and think "I never lived my life. I never did any of the things I wanted to do...." They are slow to change and tend to measure things in years and decades. Conflict is extremely uncomfortable for Type Nines. In order to avoid it, they often become passive aggressive or stubborn.

 Type Nine Gifts to the World

Type Nines offer the world peace and understanding. They value a harmonious, smooth environment and will work hard to achieve that for the rest of us. Gifted listeners with a soothing presence, Type Nines can mediate and heal the most acrimonious situations. Sometimes described as the most powerful type in the Enneagram, when Type Nines find their own center and advocate from a point of personal strength, they can move mountains through their balanced, reasonable approach and influence on others.

Type Nines Typically Report

1) They Really Dislike Conflict
Most Type Nines report conflict is extremely anxiety-provoking, and they may actually give up things that are important to them to avoid a conflict. To a Type Nine, "it's just not worth it." They usually report that in the rare instances they are willing to engage in or even initiate a conflict, it is on the behalf of someone else.

> *"Conflict makes me anxious, and I feel like I almost vanish in the face of a serious conflict. Harmony, on the other hand, feels like security. I'm sensitive to it and try to cultivate harmony around me, even in situations that don't directly affect me."*

2) They Procrastinate
Type Nines are famous for their procrastination and putting the unimportant things ahead of the important things. They typically put the needs of other people ahead of their own and put unimportant things ahead of important things. This dissipates and reduces their energy for their own goals. Sloth is considered the Type Nine vice, and Type Nines often need the pressure of a deadline to be moved to action on important things.

> *"I knew I was a Type Nine when I had a day with a long list of errands to do. I was really efficient that day and completed about 15 of the 20 things on the list. And I when I looked at the last 5, I realized they were things that were just for me, no one else. It is really easy for me to put myself at the bottom of the list…"*

> *"Doing things that are important to me is a real challenge. I know what I want, but I don't take action to do it. When I really unpackage my inaction, I think it is a fear of disappointment. I've gotten so used to being ignored or not getting what I want that the thought of setting myself up for another disappointment is hard, even painful."*

3) They Rarely Feel Anger Real Time
Type Nines experience a delayed reaction to anger and rarely get angry in the moment when something upsetting occurs. This doesn't mean they don't get angry—it just often

gets repressed for weeks, months or even years. The expression of anger works differently for different Type Nines. Some don't actually feel the anger until much later, and some feel it but repress it. Almost all Type Nines report a long delay in expressing anger about something upsetting to them.

> *"The anger needs to build up to a point where I feel like it is really worth it to say something. This can last for long periods of time. I recognized I was growing when I started to get angry a few days after an upsetting event. This was a big improvement as it used to take months or even years..."*

 ## Tools for Compassion If You Have Type Nines in Your Life

1) Ask Them About Themselves
Type Nines have a soothing presence and a non judgmental attitude that makes them gifted listeners. However, Type Nines rarely turn the attention back to themselves. It is important not to take advantage of their listening skills and to ask them about themselves.

2) Recognize Quick Decision Making Can Be Hard for Them
Type Nines consider many different perspectives when making decisions. As such, their decision-making process can feel very slow. They weigh the perspectives of all the relevant parties and try to judge the larger implications, always with an eye towards maintaining harmony. They don't like to be pressured and pushing them to try to decide quickly is usually ineffective and counterproductive. They often become passive aggressive.

3) Understand that Change is Hard for Them
Type Nines value harmony as the top priority, and they merge with their environment as a strategy to maintain harmony. Change involves uncertainty and inherently requires severing ties with at least some parts of the environment. This can feel like loss and is extremely uncomfortable and anxiety-provoking for Type Nines. Since it makes them so uncomfortable, they spend a lot of time and energy weighing the pros and cons of change, with a tendency to over assign importance to the elements that support the status quo. Many Type Nines will stay in dysfunctional situations (jobs, relationships, environments) much longer than other types. This is because the experience of change is so uncomfortable for Type Nines.

In the Body (The Energetics of Type Nine)

1) Slothfulness, lethargy and low energy are somatic issues most Type Nines experience. This type often has a hard time getting started and staying focused. They have a tendency to space out. A powerful breathwork practice that builds their energy can be really beneficial.

2) Type Nines are a body type that habitually numb out. They do this by disconnecting from their body through overeating, drinking to excess, and by engaging in low energy activities (for example, watching TV). These are all forms of numbing out or narcotization and serve to allow Type Nine to avoid right action. Any regular, disciplined physical activity that grounds Type Nines back into their body is helpful.

3) While Type Nines don't usually feel direct anger real time, they feel a tension or energetic resistance in their body when something has made them angry. Noticing this tension can be the first step to recognizing repressed anger.

Next Steps If You are a Type Nine

1) Don't wait for a problem to "disappear" with time
As a Type Nine, you have a tendency to do nothing when you are faced with a problem or when you want change. Inertia runs strong, and your mind often starts weighing all the reasons doing nothing is the best response. However, as you know, problems don't disappear by themselves. Instead, take the first small step to correct it.

2) Notice when you begin to procrastinate
As a Type Nine, it is easy for you to put the small things ahead of the big things. This is an unconscious mental strategy to stay disconnected from your power. As a Type Nine, it is important for you to learn to discern right action from action. Cultivating an awareness of the tendency to put small things before big things is the first step towards breaking the habit.

3) Try to tune into your anger
Type Nines have difficulty feeling anger real time so try to notice if you are repressing feelings of anger. The first step can be to try to notice tension or rigidity in your body. When you notice the physical marker, try to reflect back to what might have upset you.

Take It a Step Further...

The Wings

9w8: The Referee
Type Nines with an Eight wing are typically more action-oriented, aware of power and power dynamics and can be more blunt than their One wing counterparts. The Eight wing brings a directness, a pragmatism and a focus on goals.

9w1: The Dreamer
Type Nines with a One wing are typically more principled, simple, understated and graceful than their Eight wing counterparts. The One wing brings a sense of mission, an orderliness and a sense of virtue.

Stress and Security Points

Stress Point for Type Nine → Type Six, the Loyalist/Skeptic/Doubter
When Type Nine is under stress, they go to Type Six, the Loyalist/Skeptic/Doubter. This makes their behavior more anxiety-driven, doubtful and insecure. They start to worry and imagine negative scenarios. In this environment, they become indecisive and have great difficulty making clear decisions.

Security Point for Type Nine → Type Three, the Achiever/Motivator
When Type Nine is feeling relaxed and expansive, they go to Type Three, the Achiever/Motivator. They engage in right action, become focused and productive and actively pursue their goals.

The Subtypes

Self-preservation Nine: "Appetite"
The self-preservation Type Nine expresses a drive for harmony and merging through physical comfort. This is a person who enjoys food, drink, a comfortable environment and regular routine activities. Self-preservation Type Nines project their attention away from their deeper needs and direct them to a more basic, survival level. They tend to be concrete people more interested in the physical world than in abstract or metaphysical concepts. These are people who live life in a simple, direct way. This is the most introverted of the three Type Nines. They have the title "Appetite" because merging of their identity with the fulfillment of these simple needs.

Social Type Nine: "Participation"

The social Type Nine expresses a desire for harmony and a drive to merge through groups and group participation. To the outside world, this is a person who is friendly, talkative, sociable and who often devotes considerable time and energy into supporting his or her chosen group. Internally, this person often has a feeling of being different or not fitting in, so he or she feels a need to work harder and to be more supportive, almost as the price of admission. They have the title "Participation" because of a tendency to prioritize the needs of the group over their own needs and because of their drive to participate in their chosen group.

Intimate Type Nine: "Fusion"

The intimate Type Nine expresses a desire for harmony and a drive to merge through connection with a few intimate others. This is a person who uses relationships to get a sense of being or belonging. For this type, it can feel threatening to be alone. To the outside world, this is a very kind, tender, sweet, unassertive person. They tend to be very tuned into the needs, concerns and emotions of the people close to them. Internally, these Type Nines can have a lot of inner confusion and a sort of melancholy. They struggle to find their own internal compass and can have a special sensitivity to the moods and emotions to important people in their lives. They have the title "Fusion" because of their tendency to fuse to important people in their lives.

The Kundalini Yoga Kriya and Meditation for Type Nine

"You are very powerful, providing you know how powerful you are."
~Yogi Bhajan

Kriya: The Wake Up Series
Meditation: Breath of Fire

Type Nines typically struggle with procrastination, lethargy and initiating change in their lives. A growth opportunity for Type Nine is to wake up from their sleepwalking and to start actively pursuing their goals.

The Kundalini Yoga kriya the Wake Up Series is designed to be short, sweet, powerful and to help you wake up, both physically and metaphorically. Stretch pose strengthens the third chakra, the core/navel center, which energetically is your power center. Having a strong core/navel center helps you follow through on your goals. Ego eradicator strengthens the nervous system, making change less stressful.

The meditation and breathing technique, Breath of Fire, has the benefits of strengthening the nervous system and getting the body fired up and ready for action.

Kundalini Yoga Kriya for Type Nine
The Wake Up Series

Tune In:
Sit in Easy Pose with your legs crossed, bring your hands together in Prayer Pose at your heart center. Tune in and center yourself by chanting "Ong Namo, Guru Dev Namo" three times (see Tuning In on page 32).

6 inches
(15 centimeters)

Exercise 1:
Stretch Pose with Breath of Fire

Posture/Mudra	Breath	Full Time	1/3 Time
Lie on the back and push the base of the spine into the ground. Bring the feet together and raise the heels 6 inches (15 centimeters) off the ground. Raise the head and shoulders 6 inches (15 centimeters) off the ground. Stare at the toes with the arms stretched out pointing towards the toes. Palms face down and arms angle slightly out from the body.	Breath of Fire	1:00-3:00 minutes	1:00 minute*

* time is not reduced to less than 1:00 minute

Exercise 2:
Nose to Knees with Breath of Fire

Posture/Mudra	Breath	Full Time	1/3 Time
Bend the knees and clasp legs with arms, raising the heads so that the nose comes between the knees. Hold the position.	Breath of Fire	2:00 minutes	1:00 minute*

* time is not reduced to less than 1:00 minute

Exercise 3:
Spinal Rock

Posture/Mudra	Breath	Full Time	1/3 Time
In the same position, rock back and forth on the spine from the top of the spine to the tailbone.	Let the breath self regulate.	1:00 minute	1:00 minute*

* time is not reduced to less than 1:00 minute

ENNEAGRAM TYPE NINE **THE PEACEMAKER/MEDIATOR**

Exercise 4:
Ego Eradicator

Posture/Mudra	Breath	Full Time	1/3 Time
Sit in Easy Pose, fingers are pressed into the mounds of the hands, arms at are 60 degrees.	Breath of Fire	2:00 minutes	1:00 minute*
Total Time		6:00 to 8:00 minutes	4:00 minutes

*time is not reduced to less than 1:00 minute

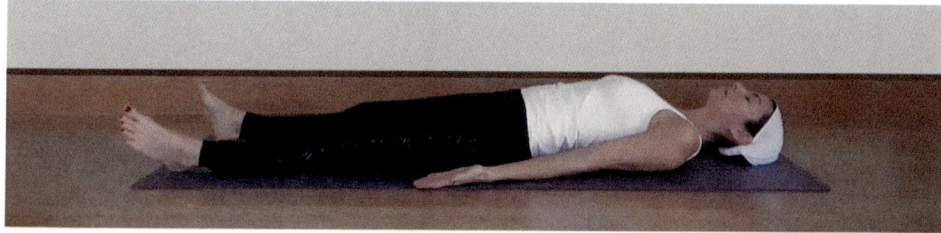

Deep Relaxation:

After you complete the Kundalini Yoga kriya, take a deep relaxation. This is when your body does its deep healing and incorporates some of the energy you have generated through the exercises. The relaxation can last anywhere from two to eleven minutes. To take a deep relaxation, lie on your back with your arms at your sides, palms facing up and relax completely.

HEADSTART FOR HAPPINESS

Kundalini Yoga Meditation for Type Nine
Breath of Fire

Posture:
Sit in Easy Pose with a straight spine, chin in and chest out.

Mudra:
Hands are in Gyan Mudra (index finger and thumb touching). Hands are at knees, palms facing up.

Eyes:
Eyes are closed.

Breath:
Breath of Fire is a rapid breath through the nose where you pump your navel point. It is rapid, rhythmic and continuous. The breath is equal on the inhale and the exhale with no pause between them (approximately 2-3 cycles per second). It is practiced through the nostrils with the mouth closed.

ENNEAGRAM TYPE NINE **THE PEACEMAKER/MEDIATOR**

- Breath of Fire is powered from the Navel Point and solar plexus.
- To exhale, the air is expelled through the nose, by pressing the Navel Point and solar plexus back toward the spine. This feels automatic if you contract the diaphragm rapidly.
- The inhale comes in as part of relaxation rather than through effort; the upper abdominal muscles relax, the diaphragm extends down, and the breath naturally comes in to fill the vacuum created by the exhale.
- The chest stays relaxed and slightly lifted throughout the breathing cycle. When done correctly, there should be no rigidity in the hands, feet, face or abdomen.

Time:
Start at 3 minutes per day and work up to 11 minutes a day.

To End:
Inhale powerfully and relax.

Effects:
Breath of Fire purifies the blood, expands the lung capacity and strengthens the nervous system to deal with stress. It gives the body a burst of energy. Some tingling, traveling sensations and lightheadedness are completely normal as your body adjusts to the new breath and new stimulation of the nerves. Concentrating at the Brow Point may help relieve these sensations. Sometimes these symptoms are the result of toxins and other chemicals released by the breath technique.

"There are two ways to change things:
Either you are forced to change or you have
the intuition to change."

~Yogi Bhajan

CLOSING

Catalyst: *a person or thing that triggers an event or change.*

In order for something to change, the current state has to be dissolved or loosened. Old habits and patterns must be dropped for new habits and patterns to emerge.

You've now seen your map out of the wilderness through the Enneagram, and you've been given access to supplies to help you on your journey through Kundalini Yoga. But there are many steps along your way, and a map and energy aren't enough. You still need to move.

"If you don't like where you are, move. You are not a tree."
~Unknown

Yogic science suggests that the number of days of repeating the same kriya or meditation has a specific effect:
- 40 days breaks an old habit
- 90 days clears the subconscious mind and builds new habits
- 120 days cements the new habit in your daily life
- 1,000 days creates self-mastery

After you identify your Enneagram type, you can practice your Type kriya and meditation for 40, 90, 120 or 1,000 consecutive days. This daily practice will help you relax your habit of attention that was uncovered through the Enneagram. Once your habit of attention is relaxed, you have the space of choice to act, rather than to react and to choose your behavior. And you can begin to hear the voice of your soul.

I wrote this manual to share what has worked for me. I had known about the Enneagram for many years before I began the practice of Kundalini Yoga. I knew my Enneagram type and my habit of attention. I found the system really helpful in understanding my own behavior and the behavior of people around me. But despite this knowledge, I was having a very hard time relaxing my habit of attention. I was making progress, but it was going slowly.

Through a completely different set of life circumstances, I came to Kundalini Yoga in 2007. Within about six months of regular practice, I found I could drop many of the habits I had been trying to lose for years. It happened almost automatically, without the anxiety and discomfort I had experienced before. Eventually I changed everything, leaving my San Francisco Bay Area life as a Certified Public Accountant to move to Athens, Greece to become a Kundalini Yoga and Enneagram instructor. Change is possible. You just need a good map and good supplies.

"Creation is ready to serve you, if you just be you."
~Yogi Bhajan

Thank you

A big thank you to all the people who made this book possible including:

- The hundreds of people who offered their personal experience through Enneagram narrative tradition panels, through Typing interviews and through personal discussion.

- All the Kundalini Yoga teachers who, for generations, have carefully passed on the Kundalini Yoga kriyas and meditations in their pure form.

- All of my friends, family and community who participated in the creation of this manual in numerous ways.

Specific thank you to the following people (in alphabetical order):

Alexander Giannakos, Amaryliss Fragos, Angie Dede, Athena Lambrinidou, Beatrice Chestnut, Bethany Chamerlain, Camille Plantaz, Camille Ramani, Carol Korycinski, Costa Tzavaras, Corinna Fanara, Daphne Kalafatis, Ekstasy Karakitsou, Elena Tzavara, Emily Krajniak, Eric Enders, Eric Roulo, Faye Fyock, Flora Papadopoulou, Ghislaine Ho-Nhut, Hans-Jorg Werling, Helen English, Jenn Hwang, Jennie Chuang, Jessica Volbrecht, Ioanna Retzoula, Ioulia Kirikou, Kent German, Konstantinos Charantiniotis and everyone at Bhavana Yoga, Kristin Tieche, Luciano Topp, Maria Kardasilari and the entire Kardasilari family, Maryam Rezaei, Muge Konuralp, Nikos Kyriazidis, Ramesh Goonetilleke, Siri Neel Khalsa, Stelios Zacharias, Virginia Moutlia.

And a very special thank you Siri Vedya Singh, my first Kundalini Yoga teacher.

- Photo Credit for the Closing Photo: Path out of the woods, Costa Tzavaras

- Photo Credit for About the Author Photos: Sakis Androutsopoulos

- Graphic Design, Book Design and Cover Art: Ioulia Kirikou

About the Author

Lynn Roulo is an American Kundalini Yoga and Enneagram instructor living in Athens, Greece. She teaches a unique combination of the two systems, combining the physical benefits of Kundalini Yoga with the psychological growth tools of the Enneagram.

She received her Kundalini Yoga teaching certification from the Guru Ram Das Ashram in San Francisco, California and began her teaching experience at homeless shelters throughout San Francisco. In 2009, she started the Rasayan Center, a Kundalini Yoga studio in San Francisco's financial district. In February of 2012, she relocated to Athens, Greece. She currently teaches throughout Europe and the United States.

Her study of the Enneagram System of Personality began in 1995. She is certified as an Enneagram Professional Trainer (EPTP program), and her training includes the Enneagram Intensive, Foundations of Spiritual Method, Subtypes, and the Enneagram Typing Process. While living in San Francisco, California, she participated in numerous narrative tradition panels with facilitators including Helen Palmer and Peter O'Hanrahan.

About Kundalini Yoga:

"I like Kundalini Yoga because everyone can do it. I usually refer to it as the yoga for people who think they can't do yoga. If you can breath, you can do Kundalini Yoga."

About the Enneagram:

"I think of it as a tool for compassion. When you start to understand yourself and your own behavior, you can start to break the patterns that don't serve you and choose you actions instead of just acting out your habit. And when you begin to understand what is going on in other people's minds, all that crazy behavior doesn't seem so crazy."

My Story

I spent most of my adult life as a Certified Public Accountant (US CPA) working in the Silicon Valley/San Francisco technology start up and venture capital industries. In 2012, I decided to move to Athens, Greece.

My reasons for moving were purely intuitive. I'm not Greek by heritage, I had no job here, I didn't speak any Greek, and there was no Greek man in the picture. I just had this really clear feeling, almost like a calling, that I should go to Greece.

And so I came.

I remember getting on the plane to leave San Francisco. My dog and two cats were in cargo below, and I had packed a suitcase full of clothes. Almost everything else I had sold or given away. There wasn't anyone to meet me in Athens because I didn't really know anyone. But it was one of the calmest moments of my life. I was totally sure I was making the right choice. And I haven't regretted it at all. I love Greece.

To access the video series, schedule an Enneagram Typing interview or learn more about the Enneagram or Kundalini Yoga, contact Lynn at lynn@lynnroulo.com.

References
Yogi Bhajan Quotes

Quote	Reference
"You owe it to yourself to be yourself."	Yogi Bhajan lecture at Master's Touch Teacher Training July 22, 1996
"Deep relaxation is not just the absense of movement. It brings profound relaxation to the physical body, allowing us to enjoy and consciously integrate the mind-body changes which have been brought about during the practice of a kriya. We may sense the extension of the self through the magnetic field and the aura."	Library of Teachings Aquarian Teacher Level One Instructor Yoga Manual page 117
"Stress is when an outside pressure is not matched and overcome by your inside intelligence."	Yogi Bhajan lecture, April 10, 1980
"Share your strengths, not your weaknesses."	Yogi Bhajan KWTC lecture, July 1, 1992
"You have to be you and that can only happen if you love yourself."	Yogi Bhajan lecture at Master's Touch Teacher Training July 22, 1996
"You cannot make your life a reaction to others; you must make your life your own."	Yogi Bhajan lecture, July 21, 1981
"The moment you touch your soul, you come fearless."	Yogi Bhajan lecture July 12, 1984
"You are very powerful, providing you know how powerful you are."	Yogi Bhajan lecture, September 28, 1969
"There are two ways to change things: Either you are forced to change or you have the intuition to change."	Yogi Bhajan lecture at Meditation course, May 11, 1990

Kundalini Yoga Kriya and Meditation References

Kriya	Reference	Author	Lecture Date (when available)
Heart Connection	Library of Teachings	Yogi Bhajan	March 12, 1986
Balancing Praana and Apaana	Praana Praanee Praanayam, page 8	Yogi Bhajan	November 7, 1984
Balancing the Head and Heart	Kundalini Yoga for Youth and Joy, page 52	Yogi Bhajan	
Strengthening the Aura	Library of Teachings Aquarian Teacher Level One Instructor Yoga Manual, page 349	Yogi Bhajan	
Balance and Recharge the Nervous/Immune System	Library of Teachings	Yogi Bhajan	March 23, 1987
Emotional and Mental Balance	Library of Teachings	Yogi Bhajan	July 21, 1977
To Purify the Self	Kundalini Yoga Sadhana Guidelines, 2nd Edition, page 12	Yogi Bhajan	
To Open the Heart Center	Transformation Volume 2, page 46	Yogi Bhajan	
Wake up Series	Meditation as Medicine, page 147	Dharma Singh Khalsa	

Meditation	Reference	Author
Burn Out Inner Anger	Praana Praanee Praanayam, page 147	Yogi Bhajan
Calm Heart	Library of Teachings Aquarian Teacher Level One Instructor Yoga Manual, page 395	Yogi Bhajan
To Change the Ego	Library of Teachings	Yogi Bhajan
Inner Conflict Resolve	Library of Teachings Aquarian Teacher Level One Instructor Yoga Manual, page 392	Yogi Bhajan
Wahe Guru	Waves of Healing, page 219	Siri Atma Khalsa
Self Authority	Library of Teachings Aquarian Teacher Level One Instructor Yoga Manual, page 288	Yogi Bhajan
Caliber of Life	Library of Teachings Aquarian Teacher Level One Instructor Yoga Manual, page 389	Yogi Bhajan
One Minute Breath	Library of Teachings	Yogi Bhajan
Breath of Fire	Library of Teachings	Yogi Bhajan

Lynn
enneagram & kundalini yoga

Lynn
enneagram & kundalini yoga

Headstart For Happiness weaves together the Enneagram System of Personality with Kundalini Yoga as taught by Yogi Bhajan to create a guide book for deeper understanding of yourself and the world around you.

This guide book leads you through the personalities in your life—your own personality and those around you, focusing on the unique strengths and gifts each type has to offer the world. Providing you with tools for compassion, this book offers a path to a more harmonious, peaceful world. If you believe most conflict in the world is based on misunderstandings, this book is for you.

Headstart For Happiness includes:
- An Enneagram type overview for each of the nine distinct personality types.
- Each type's unique gifts to the world.
- Tools for compassion if you have someone of the type in your life (what you NEED to know).
- The internal experience of each type—as reported directly by people of the type.
- Next steps towards happiness.

- A Kundalini Yoga kriya and meditation mapped to each Enneagram type. The physical practice of Kundalini Yoga accelerates the growth path for each Enneagram type.

Rooted in the narrative tradition, this guide draws on over 100 panel interviews in which people of each Enneagram type describe their experience as their specific type. Based on the idea that nothing is more powerful than someone talking about their direct, personal experience, this guide book leverages the testimonials of hundreds of people. Mapping that direct experience to Kundalini Yoga kriyas and meditations to address each type's sensitive issue, this manual offers a path towards happiness.

Highly accessible, Headstart for Happiness can be used by absolute beginners to advanced practitioners alike. No prior knowledge of either system is required. Each Kundalini Yoga kriya and meditation includes full instruction and can be practiced by people of all physical conditions and abilities. If you can breath, you can do this practice.

"Share your strengths, not your weaknesses."
~Yogi Bhajan

ISBN 978-0-9971831-0-8

Made in the USA
Las Vegas, NV
22 May 2025